GLASS WILL
Anthology of Toledo Poets

edited by Joel Lipman

a periodical anthology published occasionally by the
Toledo Poets Center Press

Number 1   Summer, 1986

dedicated to Adam Hammer
(7-26-50 to 8-24-84)

Produced for the Toledo Poets Center Press by Sans Serif Typesetters (Ann Arbor, MI) and Thomson/Shore Printing (Dexter, MI) during 1984-1986.

Editing, proofreading and design by Joel Lipman, with assistance from Cynthia Lipman, John Gibbs Rockwood and Barbara Claire Kasselmann.

All copyrights remain with the original authors. Poems are published herein or reprinted by GLASS WILL with their permission.

Copyright © 1986 by The Toledo Poets Center Press.

Library of Congress No.: 84-052510
ISBN: 0-932259-00-6

Toledo Poets Center (UH5070C)
University of Toledo
Toledo Ohio 43606

Acknowledgments

Special thanks to the Ohio Arts Council, The Arts Commission of Greater Toledo, and The University of Toledo, whose financial support made this anthology a reality. Tom Barden's "A Duck May Be Somebody's Mother" was published in *Heartland Journal*, Fall 1982, and in *Mark* issue 2, 1983-1984. Alan Basting's "Getting Over the Distance" appeared in *Mark* issue 2, 1983-1984; "Letter to Joe Don Looney" appeared in *Tar River Poetry*, Spring 1980, and in *What the Barns Breathe*, Window Press, 1983. Michael Blair's "Coming Home" and "The Drive There" were published in *Entering Toledo*, 1979; "Hey Mister . . ." appeared in *The Toledo Blade* 4/27/80 and in the *Creative Arts Community Newsletter*, 1979. William Bottorff's "Fragment of A Nocturne" was published in *The Poet*, Fine Arts Society Press, 1979, and "If Rain" appeared in *Today's Greatest Poems*, World of Poetry Press, 1983. Steve Clark's "Jimi" and "Last Request" appeared in *Short Time*, Toledo Poets Center Press, 1984. Susan Dwyer's "Ungers' Ice Cream Store" was published in *Carefully In My Heart*, Keepsake Press, 1984. Marian Fisher's "the dance" was published in *Right Now*, Fall 1983, and in *The Glass Review*, Spring 1983; "walter be home" appeared in *Eclipse*, 1983. Zona Gale's "Greening," "July Harvest," and "Metamorphosis" were published in *Spirits and Seasons*, Heatherdown Press, 1982. Sibyl James' Sonnets 21 and 24 appeared in *International Poetry Review*, Spring 1981, and in *Calyx*, Fall 1982. Jane Johanson's "The Letter," "The Novelette," "The Request," "The Rift" and "Winter Set" appeared in *Loving, Leaving and Living Again*, Becker Impressions, 1980. Barbara Kasselmann's "panther in spring," "shower," "the day we hiked up abrams creek," "lunch at the lily" and "reunion" appeared in *Mark* issue 1, 1983-1984. Etheridge Knight's "A Watts Mother Mourns While Boiling Beans," "Belly Song," "for Black Poets Who Think of Suicide," "The Idea of Ancestry" and "To Make A Poem In Prison" appeared in *Born of Woman*, Houghton Mifflin Co., 1980. "for Black Poets Who Think of Suicide" appeared in *Black Poetry*, Broadside Press, 1969, and as a broadside by Broadside Press, 1970. "The Idea of Ancestry" appeared in *Broadside Memories: Poets I Have Known*, Broadside Press, 1975. Gail Konop's "The Pear" appeared in *Pudding*, Spring #7, 1982 and *The Glass Review*, Spring 1981. Joel Lipman's "The Real Ideal" appeared in *Inc* #3, Just Buffalo, 1979, *White Pine Journal* 24/25, 1980 and *Poems 1978–1983*, Ohio Arts Council, 1984. "Alone At Jojo's" appeared in *Readings From the Midwest Poetry Festival*, 1984; "my Love is" appeared as a broadside in a limited edition by Bloody Twin Press, 1984. "A Natural Death" was published in *Convergences*, 1982 and *Mark* issue 2, 1982–1983. Paul Many's "Cattle Call," "On the Seventh Day," "The Midwest," "The Trinity" and "Wise Guy" were published in *Uncle*, Spring 1982. Sections "0000" through "0010" of Herbert Martin's "The Log of the Vigilante" were published in *Obsidian*, Vol. 2 #3. Richard Morgenstern's "Pump in a Field" was published in *The Toledo Blade*, 1/31/81. Mary Ann Napoleone's "If I Could Be A Torch Singer" appeared in *Spirits and Seasons*, Heatherdown Press, 1982, and in *Mark* issue 2, 1983–1984; "Buoyfriend I and II" appeared in the *Mark* issue 2, 1983–1984. "There's A" appeared in the *Mark*, 1982–1983 and "Faggots" appeared in the *Pro Newsletter*, June 1984. Jane Navarre's "Grandma You Used To" was published in *Image*, 1978; "I Will Never Love Anyone The Way I Loved James Dean" appeared in *Calyx*, 1979. "To A Sleeping Child" appeared in *Firelands Arts Review*, 1978, *Poems 1978–1983*, Ohio Arts Council, 1984, and in *A Change In Weather*, Rhiannon Press, 1978. "Working the Concession Stand for the Band Boosters" was published in *Poetry Now*, 1981. Portions of Jeff Olma's "The Wet Deck Poems" have been published in *The Greenhouse for Poetry*, 1973, *Salthouse*, 1975, *Writers in Residence #5*, Fall 1975, *Itinerary 2: Poetry*, 1975, *Margins*, 1976, *A Salthouse Miscellany*, 1983. Howard Parker's "Puttin' on the Fat" and "Dream-Green" appeared in *Short Time*, Toledo Poets Center Press, 1984. Jon Patton's "Angels at Mount Rushmore" and "Indian Town" appeared in *The Akros*, 1981. Bob Phillips' "Hiroshima Memorial Barbeque," "Red Rowboat Blues," "Sanctuary" and "Testing Out the Neighborhood" appeared in *Greasing the Machine*, 1982. "Miracle Fabric," "Mysterious Laundry Haiku," "Rayon Shirt Item" and "Western Beauty" were printed in *I'm Not Your Sweet Babboo*, Toledo Poets Center Press, 1981. Marilyn Pinheiro's "Siren Song" was published in the *Mark* issue 1, 1983–1984. Frank Polite's poem "The Last

House in Luna Pier" was published in *Poems 1978-1983*, Ohio Arts Council, 1984, as well as in *Letters of Transit*, City Miner Books, 1979, where "Black Butterflies" and "Carmen Miranda" also appeared. Dudley Randall's "Bag Woman" appeared in *A Litany of Friends:New & Selected Poems*, as did "George," "Pacific Epitaphs" and "The Aging Whore." "George" also appeared in *The Black Poets*, Bantam Books, 1971, *Black Poetry*, Broadside Press, 1969, and *Poem Counterpoem*, Broadside Press, 1966. "Pacific Epitaphs" appeared in *More to remember*, third world press, 1971. Donna Rowe's "The Power of Love" was published in *From Inside Out*, Inmate Arts Press, 1980. Herb Scott's "Directions," "Precautions," "Guilt," "Accessories," "Warning" and "Alikis" were published in *The Shoplifters Handbook*, Blue Mountain Press, 1974. Winston Smith's "Flashback" was published in both *Modern Maturity*, April 1983 and *Golden Song*, Harlow Press, 1984. "The Wind" was published in *Footprints in the Grass*, Monroe (Mich.) County Public Library, 1983. "River Morning Vignette" appeared in *Treasured Moments*, Monroe (Mich.) County Public Library, 1984. Marisella Viega's "Flamingos" will be published in *Ecos*. Wendy Wood's "I Never Knew It Was You" was published in the *College Prize Winners*, The Academy of American Poets, 1984, and in *Telephone 15*, 1979. "She Leaves" appeared as a broadside published by Tropos Press, 1980, as well as in *Telephone 15*, 1979.

CONTENTS

Language

9	Frank Polite	The Last House in Luna Pier
		The Black Butterflies
		Carmen Miranda
19	Pat Pencheff	Poetry
		Pike
22	William Bottorff	If Rain
		Fragment of a Nocturne
23	Herbert Woodward Martin	from *The Log of the Vigilante*
31	Paul Vargo	(through the windowscreen)I
		Push Process(stop)
		caricature
34	Brian Richards	the slider is betrayed by a white dot
		removing windsors barn
		VEST ALS/IGES
		some uses of rushes
40	Steve Toth	five function calculator
		axin yuh
		librarian
		evening fishing
		MY LIL PINK SLIP IN SLIDE
46	Nick Muska	from *28(XXVIII) Sunsets and 4 All Night Taxi Rides*
54	Gail Konop	The Pear

People

57 Paul Many — Note Left To Scare Off Burglars
from *Poems, By God*
    The Trinity
    The Midwest
    On The Seventh Day
    Cattle Call
    Wise Guy

61 Dudley Randall — Bag Woman
George
The Aging Whore
Pacific Epitaphs

67 Lawrence Dessner — Eleven Ways of Looking at a Transsexual

71 Jon Patton — for Bill Kloefkorn, Driver
Angels at Mount Rushmore
Indian Town
Iowa

75 Joan Wernert — from *Country Singer*
    Her T-Shirt Read "Riverside Recreation Director"
    Winter Olympics '80
    Buddy Who
    We're Gonna Take a Little Break, Folks
    Recession

81 Mary Ann Napoleone — If I could Be a Torch Singer
Bouyfriend I and II
Faggots
There's A
Battered

87 Marian Fisher — the dance
walter be home

89 Alan Basting — Letter to Joe Don Looney
A View from the Interstate, A Lesson in Self-Defense
Visiting Middle Bass Island
Getting Over the Distance

94	Donald Keith McKivett	Chryslers & Heaven Baby Boom Disguise The Garage Father of Lambertville
100	Steve Clark	Jimi Last Request
102	Gustavo "Buché" Garay	"Fixed" Good & Proper The Used Coats
104	Anne Perry Guiberson	Don't Do What I Do, Do What I Say Woman
111	Jane Navarre	I Will Never Love Anyone The Way I Loved James Dean Working the Concession Stand for the Band Boosters To A Sleeping Child Grandma You Used To I'm A New Yorker Now
118	Laurie Swyers	Hummingbird

Place

121	Michael Blair	from *The Ice Cream Man*
		   The Drive There
		   Bond Street, Napoleon
		   Ice Cream Man(a turn of seasons)
		   "Hey Mister . . ."
		   a late night run from Defiance
		   Coming Home
		   the ice cream man

128	Bob Phillips	Hiroshima Memorial Barbeque Sanctuary Red Rowboat Blues Rayon Shirt Item Miracle Fabric Western Beauty Mysterious Laundry Haiku Testing Out the Neighborhood

134	Zona Gale	Greening Metamorphosis July Harvest
137	Winston Smith	Flashback River Morning Vignette The Wind

140	Herbert Scott	from *The Shoplifter's Handbook*
		  Directions
		  Precautions
		  Guilt
		  Accessories
		  Warning
		  Alibis

144	Susan Dwyer	Ungers' Ice Cream Store
145	Richard Morgenstern	Pump in a Field
146	Arnold Koester	Just A Boy From Berkey
148	Joe Sheffler	*Manual for a 3 Day Mountain Walk*
160	Tom Barden	Cold hard money Shorty Greenberg's Russian Turkish Steam Bath toledo poem A Duck May Be Somebody's Mother
168	Bob Tomanski	At Home

Love

171	Peggie Cypher	Pet Therapy
172	George de Chant	7 Fantasies

177	Barbara Claire Kasselmann	panther in spring the day we hiked up abrams creek shower thursday night at the great harvest moon celebration lunch at the lily reunion moving into winter
183	Donna Rowe	The Power of Love
184	Sandy Smith	Poem

185	Jane Johanson	from *Loving, Leaving and Living Again*
		    The Novelette
		    The Rift
		    The Letter
		    Winter Set
		    The Request

189	Etheridge Knight	The Idea of Ancestry for Black Poets Who Think of Suicide To Make A Poem In Prison Belly Song A Watts Mother Mourns While Boiling Beans

196	Sibyl James	from *The White Junk of Love, Again* translitics from Louise Labé
		    (1)
		    (2)
		    (8)
		    (19b)
		    (21)
		    (24)

203	Wendy Wood	I Never Knew It Was You She Leaves

Myth

207	Carrie Allen	Maximum Occupied Armor
208	E. R. Gregory	Story of Q Culture They Laughed at Sappho
210	Martin Willitts, Jr.	Ma and Pa Kettle Meet Godzilla Jesse James Becomes Bogart
213	Eugene Marino	Elegy for Colonial Press Why Italians didn't invent the wristwatch a father viewed from 800 miles
218	Marisella Viega	Hereditary Curse State Fair Flamingos
221	Marilyn Pinheiro	Siren Song
222	Margaret Weber	Silent Things
223	Ray Gene Patrick	dream #6 key west motor momma
225	Peter van Schaick	from *The Landscape Between Us is the Dream of Oceans* Mount Palomar Observatory Hydrometer Aztlan Toledo, Ohio
230	Howard T. Parker	Puttin' on the Fat Dream-Green
232	Jeff Olma	from *The Wet Deck Poems*

242 Lynne Walker   from *Big Red*
                        Dirty Work
                        Big Red Does Michigan Wedding
                        Big Red Cherry
                        The Bald People, Tony Orlando and Henry
                            Miller
                        Big Red Answers Questions Haiku
                        Coming Home From Wampler's Lake
                        Frumpy and Dumpy Spend Memorial Day in
                            Bed

251 Joel Lipman   from *Translitics*
                        The Real Ideal
                        Alone at Jojo's
                        My Love is
                        Anne Frank
                        Low Priced Romance
                        A Natural Death

259 Contributors Notes

. . . . .

illustrations and cover by John Gibbs Rockwood.

A General Comma to America

by Adam Hammer

I wonder if it's possible
to write a poem that is perfectly clear
After all, poetry *is* a sort of mist
No one *really* understands the way his work is ignored
The world is always ready for a new way of ignoring
 contemporary poetry
And yet, the next time a poet says to you
"My latest poem describes the beauty I found in the tragic
 poverty of Mexico,
you should have seen it, those little, hispanic, tragic, vile,
 sordid,
bashful, disgraceful, radiant, disgusting, Mexican families,"
you *will* read that poem
And maybe it *will* be perfectly clear, but I doubt it,
unless the poem is entitled "The Man Who Tied His Shoes,"
but in that case the poem won't be very clear, after all,
who in Mexico bothers to tie his shoes? (Are there shoes
 in Mexico?
I doubt that too. O yes, the bullfighter was wearing shoes —
no, they were slippers. Ha! The president of Mexico
 could have been
wearing shoes, but who cares about him?
What has he to do with beauty or poverty?
I don't know, I haven't written that poem. Is that clear?
Is it clear that when I say "suicide"
many who hear me will think of death? How strange
 and wondrous
the associative qualities of language are!

We're all so busy writing normal honey
we pay no attention
to the ancient or the elderly
We never sit down with a good book, like, "Who's Who
 Among The Dead,"

or take the time to look up and see something moving—
 what is that
thing moving overhead? It could not be a kitten, of this
 I am sure
It's . . . it's a . . . O, look how clear! It's a contemporary
 poem!
O God, yes, such clear waves! I am obligated now to look
 across the lake
if there is a lake (if not, to look across something else,
 something blue)
and begin to make out little dots
in the distance
which will become waves and swallows. I do indeed
feel something moving and touching,
so moving that I begin to cry large, lace tears
so touching that I feel a large, lace wave
of emotions, a motionless wave
a wave that sweeps me back
inside to my desk, where there is an eraser,
of course. So, beginning with the last word of this poem,
which will be cloudy,
erase this poem
But consider the order in which you erase this poem
Consider how a poet would erase this poem
Consider how a swallow would erase this poem
Consider how a district attorney would erase this poem
Consider, too, how a lobster would erase this poem
(would it?)
Consider how your wife would erase this poem (if she ever
 saw it)
Consider the way the wind will eventually erase this poem
Consider the condition of the world in the year 3000
Consider, carefully, the condition of the Dark Ages:
dark, and cloudy

Introduction

As submissions responding to my call for poetry began to pour in, I realized GLASS WILL was a larger, far-more-difficult task than first assumed. I'd guessed two or three dozen poets would merit publishing, that I'd alphabetize the writers after selecting the best work, have the book typeset, printed and distributed. How naive. Instead, I heard from eighty-some writers, received nearly a thousand pages of poetry, some of it timorous, trite and tired, but mostly poems both interesting and well-crafted. The volume's objectives were suddenly elusive, given such expansive response. Should I anticipate who'd be the readers of GLASS WILL and try to compose an anthology with a vague sense of audience in mind? Or, should I assume, as an archival librarian had hinted in recent conversation, that all independently published poetry was the domain of a literary elite, though poetry's particular elite overlapped with popular culture and lacked fixed, particular socio-economic characteristics. If I accepted this librarian's theory, it meant that GLASS WILL, like so many other poetry books, would end up in the hands of a select few literati and I sought a far broader, more democratic readership. What was the best way to unite the poetry of naive writers with the polished work of crafty academics? And how would I successfully structure a volume printing work by over fifty writers, some represented by many pages of poetry, others by, perhaps, a single, short poem?

I read, reread, and re-reread the submissions. No categories, not even helpless, bland alphabetizing, would satisfy all the poets — alphabetizing I dismissed because it provided no handle for readers, no entry to the poems other than a sequence of authors' names. Traditional academic labels (ballad, narrative, lyric, visual) set off a chain of stock responses and lent an air of scholarly bookishness to GLASS WILL that falsified the freewheeling, renegade spirits possessed by many of the included writers. I didn't want readers to be told, mistakenly, and for the umpteenth time, that poetry meant forms and types, that it was most appropriate to approach poetry by first determining traditional arrangements of line or by making distinctions between narrative and dramatic intent. The subdivisions I've used (*language, people, place, love, myth*) have shortcomings and moments of awkward inclusion; however, they give the reader an opening to each poet's work that provides a key to some significant element of the poem's language, passion, subject or theme. But, these categories are imperfect and I'll ask your indulgence and recognition of the fact that it's ultimately impossible to schematize the products of imagination. Several writers submitted poetry of great variety, delightfully defying neat arrangements. One friend's suggestion was that I simply begin with "Mandrake gestures hypnotically!" and let it go at that. Not a bad idea.

All poets are enchanted by *language* and its endless potentialities. The nine writers in this section break, bend, balance and tip words and lines in varied, intriguing patterns. Throughout the section, one discovers musical, painterly, and kinetic approaches to poetic composition, and, though some are minimalists and others committed to denser language, there is an attention to words that provides the reader with delight and fresh association. *people* is GLASS WILL's largest section; these poets, perhaps no less concerned with language than those in the first section, find the jewel center of their work in the complexities of humanity. It is a section of great diversity. Under *place* one finds writers concerned with locale, land—urban and rural, workplace and home. Understandably, there is a Toledo focus to many of these poems (and to numerous poems throughout GLASS WILL). Because this city is central to the book, this section is at its center. Ecstasy, longing, passion, sexuality and eroticism are constants in the poems of *love*. There is something of the secret glimpse found here and readers may feel a bit like the guest who stumbles upon a host's hidden love notes or locked drawer of pornography. It is a physical, sexy section; at the same time, these poems reveal the vulnerable and frequent emotionally delicate nature of poetry. *myth* is the book's least unified section. Magical, fantastic, dreamlike visions abound here and it is the shamanistic, conjuring power of these poems to which a reader must be alert. The poems in *myth* are genuine transformations.

Most of these writers live in or around Toledo. Some are natives who have moved away. Four of the writers (Herbert Scott, Dudley Randall, Sibyl James, Etheridge Knight) are guests, outsiders who have visited this community — some several times — and, as poets, left their marks upon it. They have taught in Toledo area schools, been interviewed by the local media, read their work here, housed their papers in our libraries, inspired others with their skills and techniques and have helped Toledo develop an informed, progressive, expanding audience for poetry. Their work provides active counterpoint in an anthology gathered on the basis of place.

My editorial intent was to use a generous standard of "Toledo poet," not to nitpick over county or township lines, and to discover and publish the best available work. I've missed a number of writers and that's to be regretted. I have my tastes, and, as editor, rejected work another person might have included. But, you'll find GLASS WILL is expansive and broadly representative of Toledo's remarkable community of writers.

Herein are both previously published and unpublished poems. Many of those being republished appeared first in literary periodicals or small editions lacking wide distribution. I've considerable admiration for those academic and independent press editors and every effort has been taken to acknowledge those original presses and literary magazines.

The Ohio Arts Council and the Arts Commission of Greater Toledo provided grants to make GLASS WILL possible. I thank both agencies, their staffs, independent panelists and directors for their unflagging support of community literary activity. OAC and ACGT grants have been largely matched by the University of Toledo. I appreciate the vital support of the University's administrative officers, the College of Arts & Sciences, and the Department of English.

Tom Barden and Nick Muska were sometimes downright annoying with their provocative, whimsical and critical suggestions during the months I've been at work on this project. Friends are, as we've often said, "a rubber knife in the back." My wife, Cynthia, has been that essential other—I've relied upon her constant assistance, organization and clarity-of-mind. John Rockwood responded to my request for artwork with an entire sketchbook based on a reading of the typescript of this book—I'm delighted that GLASS WILL features his fresh illustrations.

Poets of Toledo—thank you for your art, your letters, notes and phone calls, for your patience. This is, of course, your book. I hope I've presented you, through your work, with accuracy, courage and fairness.

Joel Lipman
editor
GLASS WILL

LANGUAGE

Frank Polite

The Last House in Luna Pier

1

From the last house in Luna Pier
Clear to the moon
I am alone.

Stuffed with sorrow, the couch
Rolls over in the weeds
Like a huge dog.

An owl barks
Up the wrong tree, woo woo. . .

Gathering, gathering, the sea
Unravels my life,
Why are you here?
              The moon
Touches my lips with its
Spoon of salt
        And I cannot answer.

2

Old woman picking through my trash.
A grey November lace cast over
Her rags, and a hat like a clamshell.

Leaning on the screendoor, I ask
What are you looking for?

What ever is left, she says,
Treasure, redeemables. Shaking her head,
You've thrown away good clothes,
Half-eaten apples, here's a loaf
Of bread barely out of its wrapper.

I wonder who she is,
Pearl and moonstone rings on her
Fingers, gathering, gathering. . .

3

Friends come to visit,
Evening of wine, hashish, music.

Law can be poetry.
Poetry cannot be law.
Law cannot judge poetry.
Poetry judges law.

What we talk about is forgotten.

The hermit star hangs
Its lantern above the waters.
The lighthouse turns on

A pile of rocks in the harbor.

4

Unlike rivers and streams
The sea does not take sides.
It is not for human beings
To bridge for an hour's
Convenience,

Nor does it spin at the end
Of a line to nurture Egypt.
Hung on a wall, the sea
Will tell the fairest of all,
Nothing. . .

About Art or Science
Or simply where you are,
Nothing. To cross,

You must take direction
From a star, light years off,
Or be lost.

Perfect, Anonymous, Divine,
The sea reflects,
At great depth,
Itself.

And when it thinks, phantoms
Pour into our dreams.
And when it speaks, listen;
Selfish   Selfish   Selfish

5

The pen will now sail off
By itself, where love has gone.
My fingers return to my hand
Where they were born.

This is my last poem, I know it.

I grip the dark edge
Of a skillet, Ancestors, ancient,
Call me down to burnt iron, yes.
They whisper, *hard times*.
They scatter bones to show me

The way it will be from now on.

With a twist of my wrist
A domestic fire flares up. Gas is
Quick to ignite, and reliable.
A meter in the cellar ticks
Measuring my use.

This is it, at last, I'm home.
The eggs I crack
Will back up against my heart
Like unborn poems.

6

I reveal myself through a shared vision.
Now it is myself again, alone,
The vision shut down like a night
In a drunk tank.

It is lonelier than I know.
I lean closer to the earth. I go
One step at a time.

A night like this, I cherish my soul, my
Quietness. I listen to myself
Listening to myself,

And the loneliest I know is this:
The moon is a mailed fist;
The wind cold. I am delivered
Like a sand dune to another part
Of the desert.

7 Lantern

Next year I'm forty years old.
I don't know what hump I'm over.
To have made it this far, what
Does that mean? Where am I?

Where have I been? Like you,
I've been places, New York, Asia,
Great fields uncut by wire
Or river, mountains leaping up,

And O yes, oceans. I felt my way
Deeply into each, into the mind
Shafts permitted me, into
A flower (perfect on mescaline,

I laughed & wept for hours),
Into the tenderness of people. . .
I've loved, worshipped stones,
Written poems to moon and stars,

And depending on the deep and dark
Of my downheartedness, I lit
A flame in my forehead like a toad,
Imagining myself, at various

Times, Lord of Earth, Light in
The Forest, even . . . God.
Down the road with my lantern, I
Lifted up the broken, the poor,

The ignorant, the hopeless, only
To come down to this: to be all of
Them myself, at once. So what's
It all about? I don't ask anymore. . .

I am one with the insect and cloud.
I beg my life to lay me down at last,
Gently if possible, or fast, the way
A horse, plunging into darkness,

Kicks a stone out of its path.

Frank Polite

8 Luna Pier

A sea change leans against the pier
In tumult. *I know why I'm here.*
Cold streams, contending with the warm,
Grip the rocks as never before
In my life, and hurl up salt at my door.
What drifts in now is mine, cut loose,
Thrown overboard, or drowned;
A wooden spar, a bleached bone, a yard
Of torn sail like an indecipherable
Parchment. Even a shoe drifts in, kicked
Around out there God knows how long.
I listen now. I witness. I do not
Touch or twist at the integrity of each
Survival. It is enough to have arrived
At all, embodying sea changes;
To stagger ashore, free, cured of use;
Simply to be, *itself*, a green bottle,
A message delivered, a sailor, like me.

9

I promise a poem to a blue heron.

Every morning, for a week or so, it stood
In the marsh grasses outside
My window, perfectly
Still,
One leg poised in the air
As if it were about to kneel, or dip
Its quill into a blue pool,
Or disappear.

I never saw it move.

And when I turned elsewhere, to poems,
Or coffee, or pacing the room,
The heron would be gone.

That last morning. . .
Solitude of the blue heron.
Black branches of trees,
A light snow falling

Through eaves of Heaven.

10

My face inside
my cupped hands.
My fingertips
at my hairline
like soft pods
tapping the earth.
What is alive
at such times?
The night, the
silence of thought
wrapped in itself.
My skull is
a shell tuned
to emptiness, like
Love itself
before desire
created all things.

The Black Butterflies

The black butterflies of night
Clipped for sleep to nightshade and windowgrief,
Or in shaking luminous flight
On paired and silver wings, are rare
And rarely seen by human sight.

Yet, they are there, surfacing
Out of range of neons and streetlights,
Preferring underleaf,
And the dark offshores of air
To man and moth-maddening glare of things.

Tonight,
As crisis after crisis
Cracks our skies like lightning,
I think of death,
Of different ways of dying,
And of Egypt and the myth
That once held black butterflies
Sacred to Isis.

They lived forever in flight
In her private groves, compelled like
Flickering minutes
Never to touch leaf nor stone,
Never to rest, except upon her nakedness
When she moved to love.

And here is death to be envied;
To be crushed to a personal breast
Between goddess
And whatever bird, beast, lover
Fell to her lips.

Man is something else.
Myth and love will miss him
When the night is suddenly turned on,
Turned blank white,
And the black butterflies
Appear against that vellum sky
As far, flitting, burnt-out stars.

Carmen Miranda

Backstage, eating bananas
with Carmen Miranda, she offers me
her hat. I thank her and take
a bunch of purple grapes, 3 hardboiled
eggs, a muskmelon, and four
ears of corn. She says, Frank,

it wasn't always this way.
There were lean years in Madrid, Marseilles,
Cuernavaca, when dancing didn't pay
and my dear hats went unrefrigerated. . .
fruit can be expensive to a poor girl.
Anyway, I danced as best I could
with pears, beans, and tangerines shaped
from wax or wood, but it wasn't
the same. You know what they say about
a heart that wears a false face
and vice versa . . . why go into it?
It's enough to say I suffered to dance
with no hat at all. Better that
than a cheap imitation! Darling, try a
quince. Persimmon? Have a cumquat!
But the disgrace of those days forced me
to sing as an escape. And now my hats
and I sing and dance and do well.
Oh, there are times I feel all this fruit-
salad is, well, ridiculous; but it's
the thing I do best, if you know what I mean?

Before I left, I kissed her
on the cheek and said, I'm no spokesman
but I think we'll always love you for it. . .
And back on the streets that night,
I split the sky with cherry pits.

Pat Pencheff

Poetry

there is a small hole
in the bathroom screen
a wasp walks upside down
across the ceiling,
hangs full
dark like a berry

through the air
past the sink
it argues
like a hot match
in mud

the green shaving cream can reads
barbasol
menthol
beard buster,
so easily

and I notice this
just as the wasp sinks
like a raisin
in whipped cream,
spins silent
down the drain.

who can resist an accident
when words will walk
the ceiling
ripe
already falling
and sing like
burning hair?

Pike

dark twins circle beneath early stars
skirt the blue flame of water
dive to cool rings of
orange light hissing behind reeds

a water snake
on fire
glides,
small head alert
above
the water,
slips like a blade
back-beneath the surface

beneath cool water
at the far point of the lake
where the shore is opened
and an edge of raw light lingers,
long pike pass between
deep lily stalks.

my line whistles
softly through the
cellar notes of frogs,
across the last light
just above the
purple tips of reeds
searching them-
white jaw, white muscle
in the bottom jungle they displace
with clean circles

these pike are huge beneath my shadow
below the shadow of the willow
restless with mosquitos
beneath bats sliding air streams,
climbing like spiders,
sounding a web across the darkness
circling a phosphorescent
deep cave ceiling

it echoes like a gunshot here-
when a big pike breaks the surface.

William K. Bottorff

If Rain

If rain
How
Then smile
Drops on
Rose in
Very green
How then
Weep
If smile
Her
Then kiss
Me
Now then
Raining gray
And sweet
Blue
Very eyes
Love
If rain

Fragment of a Nocturne

One Willow whispers
Listens   then
Sees white hushing Moon
Harrows darkened leaves
Hears   echoes
Sparrows
And   grieves

Herbert Woodward Martin

from The Log of The Vigilante

(for Ronald and Katherine Primeau)

0000

Asientas allowed Spain to populate The New World
With black bodies stolen at random
For ducats, silver and piasters
Whisked away from the coast of Africa.
The white men came secretly across the waters
Struck their prey like lightening coming from the sky
Suddenly, then disappearing as silently.

0100

Thomas Jefferson held twenty-nine slaves
In the whiteness of Monticello.
He wrote the black man into the
Thought on his landscape of independence,
That field of white, which held all the black letters:
     /King George III/ has waged cruel war against human nature
         itself
     violating its most sacred rights of life and liberty
     in the persons of a distant people who never offended him,
     captivating and carrying them into slavery in another hemisphere
     or to incur miserable death in their transportation thither.

> *This warfare, the opprobrium of INFIDEL powers, is the warfare*
> *of the CHRISTIAN king of Great Britain. Determined to keep open*
> *a market where men should be brought and sold.*
> *He has prostituted his negative for suppressing every legislative attempt to prohibit or restrain this excrable commerce.*

Later, Persuasion deleted these words from his freedom.
Think Thomas
Of those twenty-nine
Living in your time.
You took their joy
Burdened their liberty
And let it die
And let it die.
Why do I praise equality?

0200

I bought me a blackman in Guinea
Purchased a light brown woman
And a black manchild too.
And sailed, sailed, sailed away
To make them work, to make them pay
They're worth a thousand pounds of silver
Six hundred pounds of sugar too
So if you want to make some money, here's what you do
Go to Guinea, the Ivory, The Gold Coast too
Buy yourself a man and sail away
Don't forget the young manchild too
Buy yourself a woman
Stud her with the man
To double your bounty
To increase your interest
As you sail, sail, sail away
To make them work, to make them pay.

0300

Reward Poster
I, William Burke, owner
Offer up to $150 dollars
To whomever finds and returns
HENRY MAY
About 22 yrs old
Five feet eight
Chunky build
Impeccably neat
Bushy hair, combed
Parted with pride
Ordinary color
Ordinary man
Suspected running
Towards Ohio
Offer him no food or drink
No mountain, no cave,
No woods or house to take shelter in.
He is a first-rate servant
An ordinary man
Trying to make his escape.

0400

I saw a young man who moved in anguish
O, do not pity him, do not grieve his ghost
When he died, they took and burned his body to ash
O, do not grieve him, do not punish his ghost.
As you depart, take in precious memory the most
That he gave to history: the unfettered wish
That you move among dark and friendly men, share fish,
Take bread, drink wine; remember his sores, the gash
That his body suffered, the entire length of the lash,
That he could not sit, he could not lie down,
He walked himself to death, in an unfriendly town.
O, do not punish him, do not pity, his ghost.

Herbert Woodward Martin

0500

We made fast our most offensive slaves
Bound them by their four limbs
Placed them upon their stomachs
Lashed their backs for their faults
Then covered them in gun powder
Lemon juice and pickling brine
And red pepper to remind
Them that no white man would
Tolerate their rebellious ways.
We placed their chief leader in irons
And left him slowly to die
O winds where do you push this ship?
O waters where does your parting lead?
Shall I tell you children how we lived, how many died?
By what horrendous force
We taught the body will to survive?

0600

I have felt fire sear the flesh
I have tasted the salt in an ache of sores.
O, my memories I freely pass on
It is the pain, I firmly, cannot share.

> I have seen rebellious men hung in the wind
> Until their bodies died, and that particular death
> Took revenge and punished the very air.
>
> This is the history of how "Le Jeune"
> In seventeen eighty-eight
> Bound two black women by leg and neck
> Interrogated them with fire and threat
>
> Hot lard and boiling sugar cane
> Then buried their bodies half in the earth, to attract the
>   flies.

I deliver my memories to your history, to your safe keeping.
There is no earthly pain we can share; take this song,
Breathe freely the air, I tell you this race has suffered much
That you black, young and strong might take life and not long.

0700

Call her pilgrim, call her traveler
Call her Mary, call her Sue
She knew what she had to do.
Run, Lord, run through the pine
Until she set her body free.

O, she ran in the chilly wind
Sharp enough to cut through sin.
She slept under the stars and leaves
To warm her drawn skin.
She set her mind on being free.

In the deep hush of midnight
Between the dogs' bark of fear, the master's call
She knocked up on my door.
She hardly had any breath at all
She has set her mind on being free.

I took her in, hid her between the walls
Behind my bed her body remained taut
O, I think after a while she nodded her head.
The night is a comfort to freedom,
To pleasure, to sin.

A dog will bark out freedom
And corner it if he can.
Soon it was morning and she was gone
The dogs had stopped their barking
The night traveler ran on.

0800

If I learn to read
If I learn to write
I'll entertain with hant stories
In the middle of the night.
If I learn to add
And learn to multiply,
I'll be able to subtract from
Slavery until the day I die.
If I learn to preach
If I learn to sing
I may be able to serve a brother's soul
While I put him on to this freedom thing.
The wind is in the trees.
The leaves are falling down.
I suspect a slave tonight
Is going to leave this town.
The wind is in the trees.
The frost is etched over the land.
America, you other Egypt
Hear the voice of a dead man
They lynched and butchered me
Before man, woman and offspring
They quartered by quick.
And what was my crime Lord?
What was my sin?

I wanted to walk with truth like other men
Go, where I had never been.
In that mean old town, Lord,
In that mean old town,
That was my longing
That, my sin.
I would not cry out
Not beg to be forgiven
So those men took my body cut and riven
Severed it in quarters
Burned the pieces, watched them fry

Then breathed in my spirit
Hoping they might never die.
The wind is in the grass, now.
The frost in the empty tree.
My ashes are cold and blown away.
My spirit is a ghost that's wandering.
O, America, O, your mother is slavery.
I am the bleak fear in snow.
I am the silence you ignore.
I am the space knocking at your door.
The wind is silent now.
The fire is out.
My flesh was alive.
My memory is the wind you breathe.

0900

Thirty-nine lashes the old master could lay on me
O, daughter, don't look, son don't see my shame
For after his small interval of rest
The law allows him to begin again.
O, hard-skinned master, rough as the bark on a tree
One of these moon nights I'm going to run free.
You've had your last opportunity
To lay thirty-nine lashes on poor slave me.

01000

This old land's been seeded
This old land's been turned
This old land done tried my soul
This old land done tried my flesh
How far can I run by that star?
How far will it help me to see?
Is it your fabled star of the East Lord?
Is it the constant start of the North?
Where does the light of pleasure shine?
My eyes are kept on the land Lord
My feet are to the property bound
How much freedom can I gain by that star?
How far can I run?

Paul Vargo

(through the windowscreen) I

watched a robin
bob and hop, i
watched the robin
bob
    and
        hop
(in my back yard).

i watched
     his beak
dart
      a-
round
upon the ground.

He stops,
jerks his
head
left to
    right (I
almost wonder what
he must be thinking), i

watched
the robin bob
    and
hop a-
round once
more and then

(He laughs as)
he flies away.

Push Process (stop)

Watching
(problematic)
the sepia toned
(solutions, dubbed in)
barroom scene
(conversations)
blend and sway
(fill the reels)
with unconscious gestures,
(that run on and on)
noticed by no-
(and over again;)

One
(rewind, play, fast)
time I thought
(forward,)
I saw a face or two
(pause, record all)
actually emerge
(over again . . .)
amidst the bleedingseeping
(. . . magnetic erosion)
procession that develops.
(echoes in between)

Before
(each sequence,)
my eyes detect
(each emotional exposé that empties)
motion,
(hours between record and playback)
my mind only blurs
(with presence,)
what celluloid
(memory, persistence . . .)
need be forced to concur.

caricature

the softly lit morning sky
to cry is all you need to do:

and so it seems
sends me to a place

to let your sorrow go
free it from tomorrow

i never noticed here before
a cool breeze appears

i am shivering
to make me want more

it's a form of caricature
that I hardly know.

Brian Richards

the slider is betrayed by a white dot

       like the hitters all say wait no matter
       how fast the pitch stay back
       til you see it

       the effect is a flex

       rotating still
       world hurtling slowly
       thru definite space the wand
       the thirtyfour inches & ounces of ash
       flicks it

       reflects it
       the waiting is over

removing windsors barn

                                an exercise in cultural
                           geography for debbos birthday

'the roofs fallen in. theres
nothing but junk in there.'
                         lard press
              drill press
old tools classified as   usable
                      repairable
                      ancient
                    ruint
                                    carpenters
                                    box nails
                                    in all
                                            their
                                            places

650 ft of good tin & some rough pine
sheathing still good enough
to drop from the roof
without breaking a
couple of dozen
ten ft two
by fours   trombone?!
                                                 tarnished but the
                       first expression brought a satisfying
            blatt that sat in the air as i extended the slide.
tingling lips
                 a roll of hardware cloth
                                         leather drive belts
                       aluminum cable
an arbor
           not to michigan neat anachronistic detroitus:
    dresses turned to rats nests, mouse shoes, bolts
  & taps rusted tight, just busted pails, quarter cans
 of paint, almost bald tires, most of a sled. pine stall
dryrotted to tinder.
                            a load of scrap
                                                    & it all
came home right past the troll. who passed without a glance.
how could he? thirty-year-old three-quarter-ton with a ton on
it & wanting off. ladder flagged with a lemon-yellow catfood
bag. meow mix. he must have been late for dinner.

VEST ALS/IGES

      not grasp but feels what is elected, dark
      or plain girl spine undulating in waves
      informed with variety. stretching is
      knowing as length, is measure.

§

an image of the plain girl
who has   no master
                         is at the service of all
        initiatrix
keeper of the opening shell

her
water need

not quench her cayenne fire has
always too a scepter a wand in her
sometimes in her
hand
      new moon a shell at her feet
      toward which
"copious emissions from her inner heart exude"

§

dark girl hair curls from her belly half
way down her thigh it turns
down on her

coney nipples
she is dreamy from reading from
marijuana & lingo her mind is a blade
of grass she has
runners out
seeks warmth & moisture

§

all night & all
thru today the wind
disturbed

nothing works
everything wants to pinch
this tit to come

softer but tougher than
clit sensitive to the insistent
wind high

pitched against the windows
low constant keening of aeolian ridgetops
divine wind

forced from its yearning hole
soft pussy fart to counter the prevailing turbulence

§

dark stitches
when she grins dry
blood female dark stuck up
in the hole

her words
the sibilant lisp of her voice
thru the broken tooth broke
mouth no

taut cock skin soft
enough for it

§

the elected girl

lies she
is lying in
sleep she is
dreaming in her
dream she is waiting
for what

she went to bed for
venus

is in her
body calling superior
conjunction calling
for what

she calls the sun
the center she sleeps
in dreams she waits
for

everything
she touches everything
she touches turns

to flesh

some uses of rushes

moses lay & watched the bull
rushes

vinces gangsters ran to
daylight rushes
for yardage

on the row rushes
werent like jamming the greek

of all the rushes
i have accepted dmt
was the most disturbing

pastore is ineffective when he rushes
his arm thru his delivery ahead
of his body

what the doctors call
contractions is congruent with
what some women in labor call rushes

die now
& avoid
the russias

Steve Toth

five function calculator

an speakin
        a bout
        those sons uh bitches in warshing
                              ton

        who keep jerkin
                us aghround
                      makin us
                      vote all the time away for
                      things
like
    watt the t.v. says
                as a matter O facts

their stir-tiz-ticks
        don't prove
                any god damn thing

so face it
      boy
          you ain't shit
                as far as some
                        computer in his white house

in fact
      all I got's this
             five function calculator
              that I use
                    in a grocery store
                            for balancing &
                            keeping it from
                            bouncing

axin yuh

and Those   in the midwood
       guys acting up

all ways asking
         how come? I never show
         but I ax you
              should I?
                      move from where I fit

to sum place
       wear they fight over   up next
              whose quarter's

I mean Hell
I got scruples as much
         as the next guy's butt

why they keep on?
         making me go there
                    and here so I ax yuh
     should I anyhow?

Steve Toth

librarian

                                head
                                first
                                rising
                                smoke-
                                like spiral
                    climbing
                                wet
                                    wood
                                        steps to the shag based archway and
into the library
        limited
            by the shelf space
            by the shelf life and
            by the irregular pulse motivating
    the librarian
        all nervous
        in performance of her daily performance
                            rated by those on the outside
                                forming forcasts of re-
            action from formulas pin-pointed in the graph
                                            as
                                        plus or minus
            according to the ability
                    to file the shelf quickly
                    to categorize methodically
                    to enter the code correctly
                    to facilitate retrieval immediately
                            from the current
                                    stack of neuron journals
                                    cobwebbed with the circuitry
                                    of electron poems

as those guys in the corner
discussing Escher
interrupt in-
consistant waves of
peaked and valleyed dialogue
the crests breaking her thought
                        steps
                            to bits
                                    of ionized particles
                                        in sympathetic direction

Steve Toth

evening fishing

slick
think smiling salamanders
in those yellow spotted
black bodies adhering to
vertically pen-
insular cattail
stems
all parallel

suckling weight
waving the brown bob
flags around each reed

arms ringing to
end as holder ons
holding
part above
part below
the surface
warping their shape all
content in comfortable

as those carp appear
just dead on
their hazardous territory
above the lappfull shoreline

old sun varnished plastic
smoked by
my fire I think hard
enough to hold
back you flies
swarming about the film
blurred eye
coldly aimed
at darkening sky
the other in sand

as my neon filament al-
so lieing
in that tangled wad
strung through lips
past gray gills and
further in
to rotting warm
interior decomposing
around this
rib thorned hook
snagging stomach tissue

as those foreign
treefrogs continue burping
from one hundred alternate directions

My Lil Pink Slip in Slide

Quit that
beatin your drum
all ohmfull, over-
tonefull and hollow
                      marching   the snare
                      marching   the bass
                      marching   the thud/the chest
                              the goose
                                        step
                          the canvas
                          the leather
                                              the waterbed
                                                  the heaters

```
your breasts
            your "do/don't feel like it"s
                              my pout
                              my part
                              my hair
                                              the knot now

                    HOT LIZARDS
                    of thought
                                        oh well
                                        oh sure

                                        the sweat
                                        the salt
the lubrication                                         the desert
            the lack of lubrication
                              the path
                              the plow
                              the flow

                              the vaseline
                              the stream
                              the logic
                                        the antilogic
                                              it gets between
                                              the fingers
                              in the beard
                              it soaks
            into the brow
                              like the midnight piss
                                        like the friction burns
            as I slip out of bed
                              as I slide along the floor
                                        and I hold the towel rail
                                                    to remain
                    (Ha)                   erect
to remain
                              the linoleum
                              the bowl
                              the drum
                                        in wipe out
"but it works now don' it, honey?"
```

Steve Toth

Nick Muska

from "28 (XXVIII) Sunsets and 4 All Night Taxi Rides"

(The Key West Sunsets)

Key West begins in Cleveland freezing turnpike rain
January. 14 inches of partly cloudy on the driveway
Snowshovel muscles icepick stiff and nothing moves.
Key West begins like a lover's envelope slid through
the frozen mail slot, an airticket smelling faintly
of endless tropic lust, body to sweating body,
cocoa oil in every crease, a sinusful of Peruvian diamonds,
reggae glistening centered in Walkman skulls.

Key West starts with a Midwest hijack
The shuddering mechanical airbus shaking frost
wheeling SSE, glare ice glaze drips off wings in sun.
Starts with February post-midnight blowy sportshirt
damp tropic bicycle cruise down aisles of hibiscus,
beneath bougainvillea, opening in palms.
Key West begins with a pair of 22 year old Duval Street
junkies, Georgia girls down to hassling drunks.
They pass the next pint of T-bird with old redhole Tom.

It starts with my snowshovel stiff body under 80 plus
at sunrise. Down the beach dozens of sweet blonde tits
suck in sun — midwinter marshmallows going golden.
It all starts inside me on Cleveland icy turnpike
Miles to home, 20 lbs. of wool & leather, thermal underwear
keeping us apart, seeing you step naked out of every bus, car,
plane, and train into the damp body of this tropic night.

Key West Two-Step

    they stumble to sunset
    winter citizens
    unicorns tattooed
    all over their bodies

Sunset VI

Few thin horizontal silver streamers
classic: near cloudless, clear sea air.
A Zombie in speedboat zooms pier, tosses spume.
calm: the flat, everywhere water
blue & gold glint, glass lap.
Halfsun now molten (what other word?)
into first rung of low cloud bank.
My mind's on dinner. Curried porkchops, brown potatoes.
Hardly an eye here, but
Oh, a backburnt, outrageous gold luminous flatedged cloud
blots and bleeds tangerine, silver light.

A glow, a hand above the lighthouse—
coastguard copter wheels rackety, spidery, overhead—
Now it halfs out under cloudrung to rekindle—
downpier boombedoomba congas conga—
The Big Orange slips again to the edge.
Little boaties in a line, the full rigged
Young America slides by, cameras go snapwild,
This ink runs rainbowed in eyeburn.

Nick Muska

Now the Big One's red, sunspot stands clear on it, turning
colder to the eye, now actually under the rolling water.
Afterglow comes up, first touch on the island
How everyone talks about it!
Now final fogbank halved, the last time
a one-quarter red, red balloon
Now, not a sun at all, a rust bump,
Devo hat, a melty lump, a chip
and gone.
Applause all over the pier.

Sunset VIII

Mother of pearl glows down Petronia
Sirens in distance — something burning.
In White Street Laundramat, wash swirls like soaked ghosts,
Tropical socks dry damp, muggish.
Black billows in pearly sky wharfward
While van parkers here play cassette Key-Rock.
A bug-eaten fig tree scrapes my shoulders,
Drops imagined scorpions down my back.
I look down into the night of diamond headlamps,
perfumes of February jasmine,
an iced beer to walk down the barefoot street.

Sunset IX

    fried on mesc
      blue-dot

        O

      wOw

       O,
    throw my
    gold earring
    in after it!

Sunset VII

    one
    up
    in billowing cream
    hot
    ripple butter

      §

Gay Sad Claire's
pink lit late
Marleena on the muzzy soundbox
"Falling in love again
   . . . . . .
   . . . . . .

Can't help it."

Nick Muska

Sunset XI   *801 Bar*

Happy Hour on Duval
pearl grey through
wrought iron curlicue

Bar lights come up
golden, soft

A slow roll home.

Sunset IX, Take 2

for Alden Van Buskirk

bluesinger going the afterglow
wisp long   long   bluegrey

iron boys in coastguard rig
deckride flatgrey rigid past

I remember Alden, then:

black sailors
sweating black sweat
into black uniform underwear

This is for you, then
these more than twenty years too late.

§

mid-winter summer
smell of fish
spoiled garbage
citrus here & there
frying seafood, *bollos*,
stale beer everywhere.

deviled crab   stuffed Florida lobster
shrimp & claws
conch chowder
key lime pie
beer   beer   beer
Canadians everywhere.

Tourist town:
everybody gives everybody else
directions.

Tourist T-shirt:
*"See the Lower Keys
 On Your Hands & Knees."*

Harley Biker T-shirt:
(down from Daytona run)
I'M A FUCKIN MANIAC.

30 miles shy of the tropics
the hardest choice:
to light the joint or chug the beer
to lie on back or front

another country
it's clear
sunburnt leather lips
bandana headbands
the mind turns to tofu

Nick Muska

no edge to life here
all blurs to soft focus
from drink, heat, drugs
in the brilliance
the cutglass focus
of endless blue sunlight

Sunset XIV

Afternoon by poolside,
calling themselves such,
"faggots," chatter:
"They went to Nairobi . . . "
"They got high colonics . . . "

Now, a windy phonebooth on Duval,
late dinner plans

"—a lovely, scuddy one—"

Sunset V

Ray said: "It's gonna rain like
    piss pourin' out of a boot."

    grey gloom.   no show.

    we copped.

Sunset XXI

clear   a level red west
in cabs   inhaling jet fuel at taxi stand
chasing late planes from the frosted north
misst it.

Sunset XXIII

Rush to it across the island
Atlantic to Gulf
missed by a minute
Breathless. The sky gone
spectrum gold and transpurple,
A clear raised voice after the drum chorus:

"Thank you for your participation.
Remember, you are gods and goddesses
on this blue, blue earth.
Please act accordingly."

Gail Konop

The Pear

It was still life
before someone ate
the pear,
before someone turned
off the light,
before the flower was
put in water,
before it wilted.
Still life prior to
the children upsetting
the two books
lying artistically next to eachother,
before they colored in
all the o's and a's
on the cover and left them
out in the rain.
Still life
before anything moves
when it is still
when the statue casts
shadows on the table
when the fruits caress
the skin of the other fruits,
when the wooden table
is full.

PEOPLE

Paul Many

Note Left to Scare Off Burglars

Hey you!
Yeah, you!
Read this.
I know who you are.
Does "J" ring a bell?
Think about it.
You'll have time.

from *Poems, By God*

The Trinity

So I send down My Son
To do Me some work.
(I'm gonna send the bird?)
And He comes back, the schlemiel,
With blisters!
From walking on water no less!
"Next time," I told Him,
"You want to impress people,
Fly!
I mean, I'm supposed to get
Zino pads
Up here?"

The Midwest

I like the Midwest
Everybody stays home
On Saturday night
And watches
Fantasy Island.
No trouble.
Like people in leather bars.

On the Seventh Day

In six days
I made the Earth
And all that's
In it.
Had I not gotten tired,
I'd planned:
Central heating
Zippers for coconuts
Mild tingles instead of pain
Self-trimming toenails
Lightning you could wear
Jack Daniels rainstorms
Ten-pound gnats
Two more senses and a
Third, promiscuous sex.
Instead,
You got doughnuts and
Sunday papers.

Cattle Call

There'll be a day
(Maybe soon)
When I'll give you all
A call.
And you'll have to
Stand in line and
Come before Me
One at a time.
You should bring
Something to read from.
But mix it up a little.
Don't everybody do
Hamlet.
Bring some music
If you sing.
I'll provide the
Backup on harp.
Dance?
Any kind is OK:
Tap, modern ballet.
Oh, and I almost forgot.
Bring a toothbrush.
This is a Big Production;
Plan a long stay.

Wise Guy

Yeah, sure
I heard the one,
"If God is so omnipotent,
Can He make a rock so
Big
He can't pick it up?"
Well, I'm not so bad
With paradox either.
Here,
Think quick!

Dudley Randall

Bag Woman

(For Jane Hale Morgan)

Wearing an overcoat in August heat,
Shawls and scarves, a torn and dirty dress,
Newspaper shoes, she squats in the Greyhound terminal
And rummages through two bags, her lifetime treasure.

She mines waste baskets for her food and clothes,
Scavenges in the streets with sparrows, pigeons—
Isolate, with fewer friends than beggars have—
Another stray cat or abandoned dog,
She sleeps where cats and dogs sleep, in the streets.

Sister, once did you suck your mother's milk,
And laugh as she fondled you? Did Daddy
Call you his Dumpling, Baby Girl, his   Princess?
And did you flirt with him, bending your head,
And, giggling, kiss his eyes through your long lashes?
Did some boy love you once, and hold you tight,
And hotly know you through a summer night?

Or were you gang-raped, violated early,
And from that trauma drifted down to this?
Or, born defective, abandoned to the streets?

Sister, I do not know. But I know that I am you.
I touch your rags, clasp your dumb eyes,
Talk with you, and drink your fetid breath.

George

When I was a boy desiring the title of man
And toiling to earn it
In the inferno of the foundry knockout,
I watched and admired you working by my side,
As, goggled, with mask on your mouth and shoulders bright
    with sweat,
You mastered the monstrous, lumpish cylinder blocks,
And when they clotted the line and plunged to the floor
With force enough to tear your foot in two,
You calmly stepped aside.

One day when the line broke down and the blocks reared up
Groaning, grinding, and mounted like an ocean wave
And then rushed thundering down like an avalanche,
And we frantically dodged, then braced our heads together
To form an arch to lift and stack them,
You gave me your highest accolade:
You said: "You not afraid of sweat. You strong as a mule."

Now, here, in the hospital,
In a ward where old men wait to die,
You sit, and watch time go by.
You cannot read the books I bring, not even
Those that are only picture books,
As you sit among the senile wrecks,
The psychopaths, the incontinent.

One day when you fell from your chair and stared at the air
With the look of fright which sight of death inspires,
I lifted you like a cylinder block, and said,
"Don't be afraid
Of a little fall, for you'll be here
A long time yet, because you're strong as a mule."

The Aging Whore

White wig askew above black face,
She totters on high heels up Woodward Avenue
Waving her hands above her head,
Cutting dance steps to Ella's scatting
Over radio from a MacDonald's hamburger palace.

She wears a tan blouse with belly bulging farther than her
    breasts,
Baggy blue pants with rubber bands below the knees
To accentuate her legs. No longer a stripling
In tight skirt slit to the crotch,
Or crisp, hip-hugging slacks, black men ignore her.
They can get younger trim for nothing.

She ignores them, but flags the passing cars.
Perhaps some lonely and aging white from the suburbs,
Whom Puritans have taught that sex is grotesque,
Will stop his car and bargain with her.

But no one stops. Tired,
She sinks to the bench outside MacDonald's.

A spent, wornout woman,
With vestiges of a once winsome face,
You can see why her pimp
Praised, petted, and marketed her. Now, we pity,
As she hurls hate
(Don't let no man touch you.
Don't give 'em nothing.)
In accents scabbed with obscenities
Once the darling darts of a reckless girl,
Now the filth of a young-old harridan,
Which spatters the shocked faces
Of women and school girls
Stopped at the curb by the red light.

Dudley Randall

Pacific Epitaphs

RABAUL

In far-off Rabaul
I died for democracy.
Better I fell
In Mississippi.

NEW GEORGIA

I loved to talk of home.
Now I lie silent here.

TREASURY ISLANDS

I mastered the cards,
The dice obeyed me.
But I could not palm
The number on the bullet.

PALAWAN

Always the peacemaker,
I stepped between
One buddy armed with an automatic
And another with a submachine gun.

ESPIRITU SANTU

I hated guns,
Was a poor marksman,
But struck one target.

IWO JIMA

Like oil of Texas
My blood gushed here.

BISMARCK SEA

Under the tossing foam
This boy who loved to roam
Makes his eternal home.

TARAWA

Tell them this beach
Holds part of Brooklyn.

HALMAHERRA

Laughing I left the earth.
Flaming returned.

NEW GUINEA

A mosquito's tiny tongue
Told me a bedtime story.

LUZON

Splendid against the night
The searchlights, the tracers' arcs,
And the red flare of bombs
Filling the eye,
And the brain.

CORAL SEA

In fluid element
The airman lies.

BOUGAINVILLE

A spent bullet
Entered the abdominal cavity
At an angle of thirty-five degrees,
Penetrated the *pars pylorica*,
Was deflected by the *sternum*,
Pierced the *auricula dextra*,
And severed my medical career.

VELLA LA VELLA

The rope hugged tighter
Than the girl I raped.

LEYTE

By twenty bolos hacked and beat,
He was a tender cut of meat.

GUADALCANAL

Your letter.
These medals.
This grave.

BORNEO

Kilroy
Is
Here.

Lawrence Dessner

Eleven Ways of Looking at a Transsexual

I

The technology was there so what the hell.
Life, middle-age coming, was intolerable.
The horizon was a circle closing round.
No further glory,
No more applause to deafen the echoing void.

Perplexed by the fruits of consciousness,
He reached for what he knew,
The tools of his trade,
The pill and the knife.

II

His mother died
and cut him off.
     How could she?
     How could I?
     How can I?
     STOP ME,
he cried.

III

I can take you at your word:
That body was not you, not yours.
The muscles, joyous tension of bone and thews,
Were pitched to the wrong screw.
The juices in your blood,
Roaring down through your belly,
Dancing on the surface of your lips,
Were from the wrong vial.
That surge of feeling was the wrong prescription,
A druggist's accident,
Not you.

IV

Who has not felt the same tyranny of feelings,
Felt both poisoned and starved,
Flooded and unfed?

V

The hand stiffens and shakes when we would be calm.
The mind wanders off to contemplate other moments
While the long-awaited moment passes under us,
Muddy water
With rotting slivers of belly-up fish.
The smell does not offend nor sight disgust.
The pulse winces on.

VI

How weary, stale, flat, and unprofitable
Seemed to you all the uses of this world.

VII

How long did it take your fingernails to grow,
For skin to smooth, breasts break their buds?
The voice is the same, but slower,
The bright eye and high cheek less crisp.
You throw like a girl now,
All wrist against the body's flow.
Do you sit with the girls now,
Giggle and whisper,
Tease and pout?

Are you happy now?
And has this done it?

VIII

You will be an old woman,
But never an old man,
A *grande dame* who has never been a girl.
There is one life and one life only.
No matter how it is comprised,
Yours is no more than mine.

IX

I know why.
The secret is no secret,
No disruption of the iron step
Of the mind's minuet.
You are an extreme,
And therefore clearly illustrative case,
A textbook's example,
A paradigm, not a mistake.

May you never see that book,
Nor would I tell you.

X

Has that dear hand gender,
That bright eye,
That cheek,
Crisp or flaccid?

Are you what you were?
Am I?
Was our friendship
What we may
Now
Call it:
Love?

XI

We have lived to know
That we have all been cut off,
That only God, my dear,
Could love you for yourself alone
And not your yellow hair.

Jon Patton

For Bill Kloefkorn, Driver

— 5/4/82, A.M.

They said he had a habit while driving,
that he was drawn to cow paths.
Sure enough,
he wheeled us
to the middle of a meadow.
There, as never before,
we saw the old Sun Oil refinery
backed up to the Badlands —
silver catalytic
cracking towers more beautiful
gleaming
among wild gullies and domes.

I woke to find this never happened.
But my hat's off just the same
to the driver in this dream.

Angels at Mount Rushmore

Christ, everybody was there that day,
even the lemon VW bus with New York plates
seen earlier at the Corn Palace
and Wall Drug. We turned in
between a school bus loaded with
kids from Nebraska
and a retired couple pulling an Air Stream.
Two nice young Hari Krishnas
tapped us before we got out of the car.
A sea of Indiana faces
swept over the sun-baked blacktop
from RVs to ramp, but parted suddenly
for a stampede of leathered Hell's angels.
They parked and joined the surge up
the Avenue of States' Flags toward
the gift shop and lookout.
An Angel mama, blonde with tank top,
stopped to pet a German shepherd pup
leashed to a black family.
Someone nearby was speaking French.

From the observation deck
eyes binoculared upward
to Washington's jutting jaw and
prow-like forehead,
skipped to Lincoln's. . . .
Hey, there's someone
climbing in the notch of his nose. MY GOD,
it's Cary Grant.
And above,
booming out of the low clouds,
the plump, balding man, megaphone in hand,
that must be Hitch.

Jon Patton

Indian Town

Late August
and already the North Wind
howls out of Glacier
down the rock divide
toward Dakota.

West of town
where US 2 and 89 connect,
at the information desk
of The Plains Indian Museum,
a silent copper mask—
beauty stretched drum-tight
with one blue-black braid—
files her nails.

A moon-faced waitress
in jeans and a bald
telephone repairman
tumble at mid-day
from the Browning, Montana
Holiday Inn.
In the gravel parking lot
a cyclone-fenced
aluminum mountain of empties
settles.

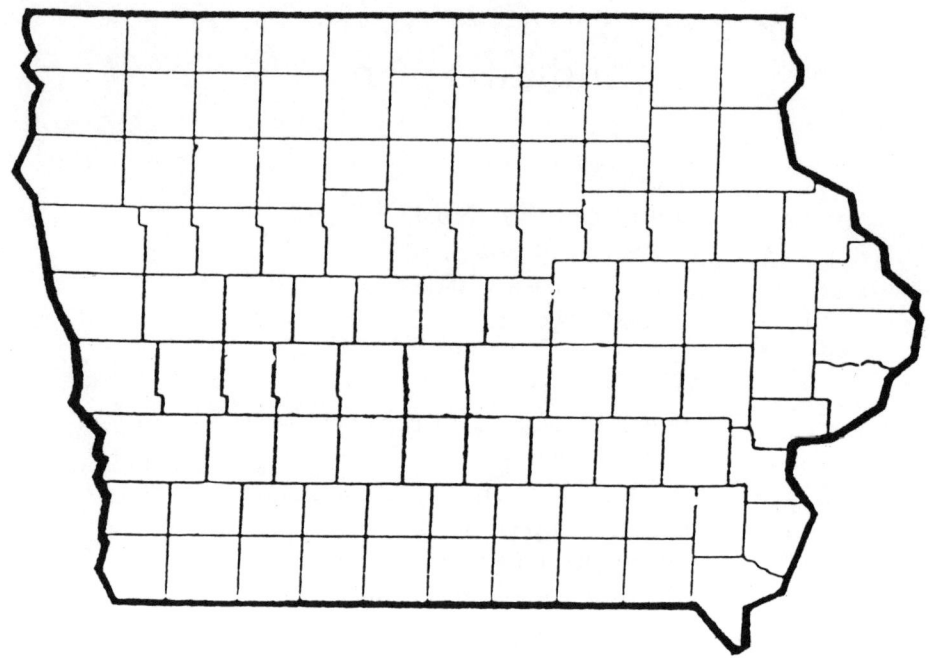

The character of its people is revealed in a map of Iowa. Every earnest Iowan harbors a secret grudge against the Mississippi and Missouri Rivers bordering the state. There, but for God's intervention, might have run straight lines, making Iowa a perfect parallelogram. Otherwise, a surveyor has been given carte blanche. Nearly all ninety-nine counties are laid out as rectangles — counties like cornfields. Two highways, one running north and south and another east and west, intersect at the center of each, and that crossroads is the county seat. There's a story in the odd number ninety-nine. Kossuth county in north-central Iowa is twice normal size. A line through its center would complete the design — Iowa would be a hundred-piece puzzle. But no, they resist a pattern clearly intended, preferring self-created imperfection to any absolute system, even an abstract arithmetical one which in their heart of hearts they yearn for. Iowans are like that.

Joan Wernert

from *Country Singer*

Her T-Shirt Read "Riverside Recreation Director"

OK, so you guys are the country band,
right?

Well, says here on the schedule
that you're on right after the
tug-of-war.

So while they're gettin' organized
you guys set up.
That way
soon as they're finished
you can start playin'.

Then when you're finished
before you leave the stage
you announce that the
softball game is at 2 o'clock
in the field behind the
auditorium.
And then
you gotta announce that the
winner gets a free pizza
from Dino's
and don't forget to say it's from
Dino's cause he's donatin' it for
nothin'.

Then you guys gotta get your
stuff off the stage
right away
cause Hugh's Dance Studio is
on next.

Winter Olympics '80

i could be home
curled in the bean bag
in front of the t.v.
watching.

instead i'm sitting in a god-damned bar
smoke choked
waiting for some drunken guitar player
to ask me to sing
my own song.

the lead and i have worked out a deal.
i do three of his
he does one of mine.
it's his band.

the bass is half asleep
and the rhythm, fresh out of prison
for beating a man to death
uses my walking time to
light up a cigarette and finish
his drink.
i remind the drummer to watch the tempo.

we start out too slow
and push and pull each other through
like walking
on tar in mid-summer.

afterward
as i make my way among the tables
a man grabs my arm and tells me
he didn't know i was a singer. i tell
him i'm not a singer,
i'm a writer. he laughs and i move
on to the bar
and the mindless blue roar of the
t.v.

the bartender buys me a drink and says
u.s. just beat russia.

"Here's to the U.S. Hockey Team."

Buddy Who?

Freddy-the-drummer
didn't show up for practice
tonight
and Mike, the bartender,
who usually fills in
when Freddy-the-drummer
takes off,
said he wasn't playing um,
cause he had enough to do.

None of the other guys
could play them and
their guitars too
so Vern told me
I had to play them.

I told him I never played
the drums before.

He said, "It's easy, just put
one foot on the bass drum pedal
and the other foot on the
cymbal pedal. Then ya just
count out the beat."

I said, "Well, aren't I
suppose to hold some sticks
or something?"

He said there aren't any cause
Freddy-the-drummer always
takes the sticks with him.

It wasn't so hard.
Sort of like riding a bike

with no hands.

We're Gonna Take
A Little Break, Folks

"Hey Wernofsky, what's with you tonight? Don't you like men?"

"Yeh, I like men."

"What is it, then? Is it me?"

"No, it's not you. You're alright."

"Well is it the songs? Aren't we playing them right?"

"No, they're ok."

"Well somethin's wrong, cause everytime you look at me I feel like I should be somewhere else."

"It's nothing."

"Are you on the rag?"

"No."

"Ya have a fight with your old man?"

"No."

"Then what the hell is it?"

"I told you, It's NOTHING!"

"You know, Wernofsky, sometimes you're a real bitch!"

"I know."

Joan Wernert

Recession

I was gonna write a poem
today.
Then he came home.
Said there was no work, things
are getting bad.

But I can't write when someone's
around.
And besides all day long
he is hammering on the side
of the house and i can't
concentrate.

Finally I decide to cook spaghetti
only the burner don't work
cause he pulled the circuit breaker
so he wouldn't get eletrocuted.

So I said the hell with it
and sat down and wrote this poem
which is what I wanted
to do in the
first place.

Mary Ann Napoleone

If I Could Be a Torch Singer

for Jane Navarre

If I could be a torch singer
I'd never write a poem
never need to bleed
in ink.

Edith Piaf in Ishpeming
I'd stand up small in smokey
clubs to sing my bluesy soul out loud.

Crowds would love me
when I'd sing my long gone loves
then lament my dowrong daddy now o

woe o wow if I could sing
my torch would scorch
like redhot mama low
down blue, indelible as long
black strokes in ink.

Buoyfriend

I.

While we talk
this afternoon away
I want to play with you

leaning close
as a son or new friend.

I say other words
for

you're beautiful
when you stretch
swat a sweat bee

talk lovingly
of your ownly niece
who's two

frown
    too late for lunch
    too early for dinner.

I want to feed you
almonds, oranges
honey.

You are so light
I could lift you
with my tongue

like a lily
or laughter

sliding into my mouth.

Mary Ann Napoleone

II.

Buoyant as snow you enter
my honeyscented house
where we fall easily
into talking

and you eat almonds
from a China bowl
as if you know

you're welcome
as February sun

slight in blue/gray
East Tennessee
on your naked tongue.

I want you to stay
because you're not a boy

I have fed you

and your company
is honest as a strawberry.

Faggots

We could have bought
our freedom with a blow job
Brother but lacking such desire
to please His Eminence we choose this fire.

Here we stand bound
to our wise sisters

one who heals
one who warns
against sugar

one whose gaze
withers the rod

one who will not ask
forgiveness from a falsebeard
fathergod.

Now wet straw smokes.
Onlookers cheer, choke
wave away black billows
cloaking us like angels' wings.

Beside us a sister sings

> Breathe deep, my dears
> before high flames reach us.
>
> Breathe deep and pray
> we end like Joan of Arc
> with nothing left but heart.

There's A

bicycle
in the driveway

a hobby horse
an ax

rage
at the drop
of joy glistening
on my mouth

    'Why don't you
    do what's right

    invite friends
    remember the needy
    read magazines
    bake pies'

There's a bicycle
in the driveway

an ax
a hobby horse

an ice star in my eye

    'Why don't you know
    where your children are

    let your hair grow
    paint your fingernails red

    Why don't you go
    to church

    Why don't you teach
    your daughter to obey'

Mary Ann Napoleone

There's a
bicycle
in the driveway

a hobby horse
an ax

a daisy on my head

Battered

Bruises never show
where hard words strike
secret parts puffing
inside like flesh under eyes
after sleep or long crying.

Mirrors within know
veindark blue as you
snap the whip tongue sharp
like a towel crack to the butt
slide away, smiling.

Mary Ann Napoleone

Marian Fisher

the dance

kasimer brings ladies
to his flat and
serves them kishka

he plays helena on his
double cleff and changes
keys like myron floren

women clap and wave their
arms and he answers
dzijkujemy with a shy lisp

the room smelling like duck
soup on easter
and the women dance

kasimer polkas like a mean bear
clawing women as if
summer sausage

and the women stand like
kielbasa hanging behind
the coal furnace
waiting to be skinned

walter be home

thirty million days
ago everyone's grandpa
came to america

thousands of sand
from europe
plain men
busha women
crakow feet
poznan ankles

packed with klusticke
waiting for god
to help them forget poland

bohemians washed their hair
in beet juice
armenians drank it

one world above the other
cantor and hail marys
kielbasa and herring
aunt margaret-uncle stashu
uncle stashu-aunt margaret

and they came to america
so we could have christmas
so quamke would never die
waiting for god
to make another heaven

Marian Fisher

Alan Basting

Letter to Joe Don Looney

I remember in Chicago
how first you dragged the Bears'
front four to the goal line,
six yards like a steamer.
We cheered hysterically
when you bounced from under
the crush waving
both shoes overhead
and smiling. We'd never seen
anyone strain himself
right out of his shoes.
Later that day
Pettibone would hang
for the last ten yards
like a two-legged flag on your jersey.

Your were my favorite maverick.
Even when you ran
the wrong way in Detroit
I thought there was hope.
You'd somehow realize
and turn.

I wanted to be
you, Joe. I wanted
to say to my quarterback
"just gimme the ball and
look outa my way."
I wanted to punch my spud-nosed coach
and yell
Fuck you Bud Wilkinson!
But I had shortcomings.
No faith in my own insanity.

Yesterday my wife
read me the article,
"Don Looney Finds Peace
with Baba." A guru?
For Joe Don Looney?
I had trouble with my throat.
What happened Joe?
I wanted to call you up
say hello and I'm still your fan . . .
and you don't need
that, Joe. Say no to Baba
and his faithful bee-bee brains.
No to the Cosmic Cruiser.
You're a mustang, Joe
and I need to know you're out there,
plagued with strength
and disbelief. Crazy
in *this* world, somehow.

A View From The Interstate, A Lesson in Self-Defense

Two sounds:
the whine of four tires resistance,
the rush of an iron block through air.

Ahead in the black
refineries burn air orange.

In the razed palace of Toledo,
harbor for grain ships and brick pods, empty,
the moon shines into a basket.

Erie washes and then washes
a black web of beach roots from the sand.

Asleep with his head on a horse's skull,
the beast of east Toledo dreams
a mountain of little glass combs.

Under eaves lined with ash
and the first sounds of rain,
children, falling in their sleep,
turn themselves into rosebushes.

Alan Basting

Visiting Middle Bass Island

for Ed, Tine & Cass

Rising from a fair night's rest
with a two-year old
tearing dreams between us,
butting our chins in his sleep,
I plant my feet on the floorboards.

This morning I'll hook the first
big bass, I whisper, disbelieving.
Sunlight dances off the cove
and the room's cornflowered walls,
echoing a cheerful domesticity
disgusting without sleep.

The first beer before nine-thirty breaks
the promise I made to my wife.
The second and third only drive
the wedge between us deeper.

But exile's what I need right now—
a spat, some confidence in the fact
that I'll be alone for awhile.
All to gain some snot-slick fish
and an hour to unplug my brain.

When the first one hits,
breaking surface in deadly air,
I dance a quick-step over stones,
delighted with my change in luck.

Working the fish, allowing it range enough
to think it can get away, I pull this—
my happiness, red-eyed, from a dark hole
green to the bottom of the lake's throat.

Getting Over the Distance

for Pete

When you were born, I put off writing
for you, thinking I was too excited,
too close to the subject, and that
was wrong. When other "writing friends"
had children and delivered their well-
crafted joy, I felt pressured
and guilty, and that was wrong.

When, after three years, still
I had not delivered, had given up
my "other life" for a wasteland with a view,
had burned a barrel of brain cells drinking,
papering the wailing wall with excuse,
I strapped myself in and lectured —
I'd never be fit for dog lime or writing,
and that was almost right.

But now I have something for you,
something I think feels right:
last night in a dream, you and I
were alone on a sandstone tower.
As is customary in these scenes, you slip
through feathery guard cables
and begin falling. This time, resolute,
I leap over them after you,
wanting you to turn your face up
to see me, see that I am on the way,
that things will be okay
between us.

Donald Keith McKivett

Chryslers & Heaven

In the midst of the mediocrity in
which I grew, kingdom of the neighborhood
was often determined by such
things as who could afford Cool Whip
at the regular non-sale price.

My father never proclaimed
reign with lucrative status.

But most any summer's night he could
afford a kid sitter and the two
of them were off! Usually an
outdoor Johnny Knorr B.Y.O.B.
dance at Centennial Terrace, or somewhere.

He'd jump into his freshly waxed
Chrysler (services provided by myself),
check his tie in the mirror, and
before backing out of the drive,
unwrap a Swisher Sweet and say, "I wonder
what the Poor People are
doin' tonight?!!"

Baby Boom Disguise

Skinny gorgeous mean lookin blac women
now gaining weight — wearin low heels — sayin Hi
to average white males in Saturday tee shirts.
The few polite long haired and bearded men around
remembering the rock stations
without MacDonalds and cold cream, and the crap.
Now drivin their girl friend's silver gray wedge shaped Olds
around, happy.

The country of the U.S. was tired of bein fat without
a profit and put its people on a diet. In
January, February, 73, 74;
The wonderful world of nine to five
waiting in line well after
six for gas.
In blac-carboned snow
nobody happy except ex-pump jockeys
ringing their N.C.R.'s.

Customers selling their born-to-die models with extended
    bumpers
that came out just a year or two before, cause the government
wanted to protect us from a five mile-per-hour crash.
By the great 200th birthday celebration in July, 1976
everybody was happy with a
$7,000 Chevette, and
paying a buck twenty a gallon.

Nothin more beautiful — nothin more disgusting — nothing
more equal than a beautiful gal bent over
her car in heels after the office — in heels
with jewelry pumping that unleaded. I'm watchin
the eighteen year old watchin. The same
kid used to clean her windshield and check the oil and fill
her tank — and she'd ignore him and drive away
with him tryin to say, "Hi".

Donald Keith McKivett

Now he's pretending he's counting
plastic 7 Up bottles as she walks up to the booth
with stinky hands to pay.

But I got too high. But I kept my crash bumpers.
Over big. Over chromed. Early
evening running lights.
Justly paid human Detroit factory assemblers.
The mean blac women and old
freaks don't really forget.
But I talked about it.   I disowned it.
I loved it.
I kept my Bi-centennial Mercury.

The Garagefather of Lambertville

Let me tell you a story of a paintin fool
who likes to have his fun,
but he keeps his cool;
changes rusty rags into Coupe-De-Villes.
He's the
         Garagefather of Lambertville!

Well, for bumpin and grinding he's the best,
and the Garagefather name
took to the west.
Then an offer came
Oklahoma way.
and came the time the boys had to say
Goodby to the
         Garagefather of Lambertville.

> He'll fix your rag and give you a deal.
> He's the Garagefather of Lambertville . . .

Well he kissed his wife and wiped away her tears;
put on his hat and put down the gears.
Headed down south with the light of the moon,
thinkin bout the words to a Haggard tune.

Cause he was tired of Donny's rock and roll;
gonna learn the steps to some Cotton Eyed Joe.
But with nothin to greet him but the Okie heat,
he stepped into a parlor to rest his feet.

A man named Rigger bought him a beer,
and eventually asked,
> "What are you doin here?"

The Garagefather grinned to the barkeep;
he returned the favor, he began to speak.
He said,
> "I been paintin Detroit steel,
> I'm fast and great,
> but it's no big deal.
> I want to slow down,
> but I gotta move,
> so I come out here
> to get some country groove."

I'm gonna make em huff and puff
at the Huffy Bike Plant Shop,
and show em what a
Lambertville paintin man's got.
You just give me some men with a lot of pride,
and I'll show em right away
that I'm on their side.
We just skip the shit that doesn't count;
we get them vehicles painted and out.

Donald Keith McKivett

Well Rigger said,
"Sir, that sounds just fine
and I wish you all the luck
on that assembly line.
Cause these boys down here, they like it slow,
cause if the boss says yes, the union says no.
And they're happy just to make their buck.
Have a good time, have fun,
good luck!"

But the first day at work
he was right on time
and the boss man said,
"Just try to paint nine."
But he had that using none of his tricks,
and by luncheon time,
there was thirty-six.
And with fifty-eight more by midday break,
by quittin time there could be no mistake.
This man is the
                Garagefather of Lambertville!
                Garagefather of Lambertville!

He'll fix your rag, and give you a deal,
He's the
                Garagefather of Lambertville!

But he was sittin up at night alone in his lodge,
thinkin bout the boy's garagefather's garage.
There's old Keith Vonn;
he's having a ball.
And Donny's D/A'n before a Prep-Sol.
And sure, Mike Queenie
can change that mill,
but that rag's a Ford
not an Oldsmobile.

Donald Keith McKivett

Well it didn't take him long that he came to decide;
that a four wheel Jeep, not a horse, is his ride.
His guns are in Toledo loaded with paint,

> A Garagefather he is,
> a cowboy he ain't.

So now,
he gets his country from K99;
in the comforts of his garage
from time to time.
And every now and then
for a country thrill,
he goes no farther west
than Bronco Bill's.

So if you need somethin done
just give us a ring.
Some body will answer
and begin to sing,
"We'll fix your rag,
and give you a deal."
He's the

GARAGEFATHER OF LAMBERTVILLE!

Donald Keith McKivett

Steve Clark

Jimi

I marveled at his mastery in Monterey
in '67
his panther black hand moving
like a streamline train across the
strings of his axe
Like a rolling stone.

I was amazed in Detroit by the vibrating marshalls
in '69
playing with his teeth
Purple Haze.

I listened in Saigon to another great masterpiece
in '70
Voodoo Child.

I watched in awe at the bright sunburst of flame guitar in
     Chicago
in '71
Red House.

I dreamed to the risingfire, on a radio, in my dark house lit
     up with
the bright colors of LSD
in '72
Machine gun.

In crept my best friend, head bent, tears
like rain dripping from his face
"He's dead!" he said
"Who's dead? That girl, who was she?" asked
Jimi. "Jimi with an i," he cried.
Manic Depression played on and on.

Last Request

I want to make love to my wife.
I want to see my son.
I want to have my freedom.
I want to see the sun.
I want to feel the wind in my face.
I want to hear the birds sing.
I want to taste a good cup of coffee.
I want some BBQ ribs.
I want to have fried chicken.
I want everything I have lost!
And the executioner says, "Any last request?"

Gustavo Buché Garay

"Fixed" Good & Proper

Maravilliosa! Erie street
. . . Donde cruza dormelona Chestnut
— Duer me!

. . . From the Maumee river
gentle breezes of a cool summer dawn
blow wild river fragrances
through the slumbering haven
. . . of hillbilly ghetto dwellers
who still dream blissfully
——— In the womb of North Toledo!

. . . a lingering, river morning mist
——— still hangs in the air!
I'm standing under the huge buckeye
by Lebanese Jimmy's carry-out . . . all alone
——— feeling supremely contented!
My right is in my pocket
fingering the last pieces of silver
——— to my name!

. . . Very early that morning
——— I'd "fixed" good and proper!
The awakening ghetto felt divinely justified
. . . Opium tranquility flowed through my veins
——— Andava llo bien "curadoté"!

The Used Coats

I am more intimate with Goddess Justice than all of you — O lawyers and legislators!

I met her at a Salvation Army store one freezing winter day while shopping for a warm jacket. She was tall and stately, shrouded with magnetic mystery, awesomely beautiful; and she also was in need of a warm used garment.

She smiled and her smile kissed my heart.

She looked at me with her large limpid pools of magnanimity and her look caressed my soul.

She spoke in a celestial whisper saying, "Your impertinence and impatience with Justice are justified before me, O beautiful child of man, partake of me as your agitated heart prompts you; there is purity in your impulsiveness, innocence in your acts, and your touch assuages the pain of wounds your brother man inflicts on me."

The Goddess slipped into a white coat, glided magnificently, out of the store . . . without paying for it!

I slipped on a warm blue jacket and followed her lead . . . This is my thief's apology!

Gustavo Buché Garay

Anne Perry Guiberson

Don't Do What I Do, Do What I Say

(Addressed to the Rapist/Killer of 7 Ann Arbor U of M coeds, July '67–July '69, now incarcerated for life in Southern Michigan State Prison, Jackson, MI.)

I am your mother. You invaded my body, took it over,
for nine months. When they pulled you out,
you screamed, covered with red slime. I
loved you anyway. I did my best
for you. But you disappointed me . . .
I put you away for awhile . . . What else could I do?
You wouldn't listen, got in so much trouble;
there were others to take care of.
What else could I do?
I am your mother
and you said
you would get me for it . . .

I am your sister. When you came to me for advice
and comfort, I told you to get out
of my room. You were a dirty little
boy, always underfoot. I was stuck sitting
with you, when I wanted to be with
my boyfriend. Dad always beat
you with the belt when I
told on you. I would stick out my
tongue at you as you slunk
back to your room.
I am your sister
and you said
you would get me for it . . .

I am the little girl down the street.
You took me out back in the bushes. We
took our pants down. You said
it would be okay. Then you wanted

to touch me. I ran home, told
my mother; she called your mother.
You got a beating.
I am the little girl down the street,
and you said
you would get me for it . . .

I am the girl next door. You found me
home alone one day. I was standing at the
ironing board, and you came in, awkwardly,
timidly asked me for a date. Laughing at you,
I said you were too young, I went out with
men. You could still hear my laughter as you
ran out.
I am the girl next door,
and you said
you would get me for it . . .

I am the whore your buddies took you to
on your sixteenth birthday. They
pooled their money, said it was time
to become a man/
You were so scared you couldn't
get it up. My cackles followed you down
the stairs as you ran red-faced past
your friends. "Next time, send a man,"
I screamed to them.
I am the whore,
and you said
you would get me for it . . .

I am your special Aunt and you thought I
was the only good one. You would come
to my kitchen for a cup of hot chocolate and
comfort. But one day, you came unexpectedly, caught
me in bed with a man who wasn't
your Uncle . . . You never
came back.
I am your Aunt
and you said
you would get me for it . . .

I am your classmate. You know, the
one in the fifth row. Your stares
caused me to blush. You asked
me for a date and raped me in
the back seat of your buddy's car. I
was in my period, and you slapped
me when you saw the mess. When
you took me home, I slapped you
hard across the face, said you disgusted me.
I am your classmate,
and you said
you would get me for it . . .

I am your wife. I tried to take care of you.
I was so young, and just learning about
life. I didn't know how to please you. Then
the babies came. Pushed you; we needed
things. You never made enough. I
guess I did expect too much; put you
down. Mom said you weren't good enough for
me. Cut you off when you didn't do
what I wanted.
I am your wife,
and you said
you would get me for it . . .

I am your lover, and you told me everything,
and still, I loved you with all my
heart. I put up with your strange comings
and goings; the lame excuses. You did little
things to make up for it. I
tried so hard to understand. But
finally, I had to let go and walk away.
I didn't want to, but I had to
save myself.
I am your lover,
and you said
you would get me for it . . .

I am your daughter. You held me
too tight when I was little, and I
was afraid of you. You hit me,
yelled at me. I ran from you, hid
behind my mother's skirt.
You would tease my girl friends,
trying to touch them. I could
never talk to you. One day, I
screamed at you, walked away; never
spoke to you again.
I am your daughter,
and you said
you would get me for it . . .

I am your victim, the girl you picked up
at the bus stop. You lured me in with your
clean cut looks and charm; the bus was
late, and I was in a hurry. You took me to that
place, tied me down, stuffed a rag down my throat
when I screamed. You
raped me, ripped into me . . . Your knife, your
penis, cut and stabbed into me . . .
Cut me to shreds, cut out my womb, breasts,
my hands. Wrapped my torso in
a shower curtain; dumped in a trash pit.
. . . returned to the scene, you were caught
as you recoiled in horror at the sight
of my insect covered rotting remains;
Denied you did it as they took
you away.
You barely knew my name — didn't even know me.
I am your victim,
and as you were killing me,
you said
you would get me for it . . .

I am the nurse in the hospital
where they took you. I
gave you the shot
that put you out. I
hooked the electrodes to your head,

Anne Perry Guiberson

pulled the switch that took
away your memory—
I was there when you woke
confused. I sat you in a chair,
made you eat egg and toast,
patted you on
the head, called you a good boy.
I am your nurse,
and you told me
you would get me for it . . .

I am the teacher who belittled you.
I am the Shop Supervisor who humiliated you.
I am the cop who gave you the ticket.
I am the sales clerk who cheated you.
I am the little girl who ran from you.

I am your mother.
I am your sister.
I am the girl next door.
I am your special aunt.
I am your wife.
I am your lover.
I am your victim.

I am your executioner . . .
. . . you never had a chance.

Woman

I am the sum total of what I want to be,
don't want to be,
hope to be, afraid of being . . .
I am always here, never here,
lending a kind word, helping hand.
Nine months curled inside
my womb; sharing blood, food, illness;
you joyfully kicked me out of shape,
delivered me into sleepless nights,
tinkly belled rattles,
musical gurgles of delight;
holding onto innocence as long as
you can . . .
You come for advice.
Teasing you, I chastize gently.
Your first love, I shared your first time;
know how awkward you were.
You are my Superman. I
take you in, all of you in,
beg for more, expect more.
Swallow you; clean
dried semen from your sheets,
gently wash all clean.
You are afraid — the power
between my legs, primal urge you feel
at my breast. You suck, sob,
attack, retreat, kill, cut
out the fertilized egg.
All you have to do is love me, love me,
love only me. My
inside aches for you, bleeds for you, doesn't
bleed for you. My breast heaves, wrenching
grief at your leaving, your coming.

Anne Perry Guiberson

You fought my father for my hand; spread
your honor to keep me dry, slave
at a disgusting, demeaning treadmill
to care for me.
You quit drinking for me, went drinking
because of me, made an ass
of yourself to impress me. Scolded
me, spanked me, kissed me, held me, beat me,
uplifted me, crowned me queen of your heart.
Perfumed, flowered, and showered me.
You sleep with me, sleep without me.
Keeping me from harm, you hold my hand as I totter
my first steps.
I am your curse, your most blessed one.
You tied me up.
You set me free.

Jane Navarre

I Will Never Love Anyone the Way I Loved James Dean

in his red nylon jacket at the planetarium
hiding out at the old mansion from that gang
no cause to be a rebel: *I* would have loved him

james—*jimmy*—with his sidelong grin those cute
glasses shucks blinks a little wave in his hair
shy shambling no football jock a poet not a hood

natalie as hot for him as for splendor with warren
which reminds me of shelley and her tragedy
with montgomery who reminds me of james dean and

there was natalie mothering poor sal as i would have:
and your kisses James! (i would have helped him too,
natalie.) elizabeth after eddie-debbie you are not good

enough for the touch of him my mattress rose
and fell alone in my room with tears for crashes
in crushes in flames of giant lovers in eden

it was the purest love i've known for love's sake
in just-15-year need the very greed for love
that's unrequired. i murmured prayers to him before

my prayer: dear james dean james dean don't be dead
you can't be dead don't be don't james do james
oh james oh. i took up with jesus soon after.

Working the Concession Stand for the Band Boosters

my 21-year-old college junior sister
just got back she calls collect
from Paris, Granada, Florence,
London, Madrid, and her classy
Moroccan/Spanish M.D. boyfriend
who looks like the guy in the Winston ad.
his name is Fernando as in Lamas

I draw pepsi and mountain dew
for children and parents in school
colors and fat bellies for the football
game oversteamed hot dogs and cold buns
stale popcorn hot chocolate hot coffee
there is a full moon tonight
fall is here and we are cold

our high school children march on the field
in the new uniforms this profit
bought them.   our foreman played trombone
for Ohio State from '58 to '61 and he *loves*
bands we all believe in opportunity for
our children i am the mother of a
teenage trumpet player

and I will never have a classy Moroccan/
Spanish M.D. lover   tonight there
is a full moon   nor leave my leather bag
at Orley Airport in Paris, France

Jane Navarre

To A Sleeping Child

you sleep.
2 a.m., the mid of night
I must flash this light
to see that your pupils
are each the same size

your swollen face
bashed into blacktop alley
your inner lips flared
with stitched tooth gashes
your scabbing cheeks

smashed nose and knees
foetal you lie
pillow covered
with a bloody towel
you cannot suck your thumb tonight

your friend brought your bike home
a neighbor carried you
home crying "mama"
mama mama mama mama
I almost cried for my own

at the sight of you
you and your trust
your arms thrust at me
believing I'd make it all
all right

as mothers are reputed to do
who else does a child have?
who does anyone have, ever?
mamamama
we own each other

Jane Navarre

irrevocably parent and child
unbinding unwinding
I know this
and am not eased
knowing it

Grandma You Used To

keep a boarding house you fed pulp cutters
and ore dock men and railroaders up at 5
each morning packing lunch buckets
changed their beds fed them dinner too
for three bucks a week *work work work*
you yelled to my mother and aunt at dawn
sleeping behind the draped arch front room
(now my mother feeds you baby food)

        Grandma you came over

on the boat to the promised land in '07
from finland to be a maid in the U.P., michigan
they beat you your cousin took you away
to the next town you were 16 you cleaned up
after rich people; work work work
you yelled at my grandfather a handsome lad
dark wavy hair who drank til you
divorced him when people didn't get divorced
(now my mother changes you)

Jane Navarre

Grandma you scrubbed

floors at the hospital a scouring maid
dumb finn and crabby lady on your knees
and hands a cow a garden and 4 kids
can't even talk english waiting on people
all your life; work work work
you yelled at your grandchildren whose mother
was having a baby on your hands
and knees scrubbing clean floors
(now my mother spongebathes you)

Grandma your mother

wouldn't marry your father in finland
she was a weaver travelled then town to town
with you the fatherless child the outcast
laughed at and scorned so when i came to you
pregnant with my new young husband you held
my hand on your knee and said *love each other*
in a language i never learned: *rakastaa:*
before you died you wanted to make for
my mother serve her just one cup of coffee.

I'm A New Yorker Now

I have 3 keys to my house.
I'm a New Yorker now
I must get locks
for my gas tank, ignition,
hood, and an alarm
on my fender. My antenna
slides in, locks, also.
My insurance is $1600.00

I don't meet people's eyes
and smile as we pass
I see fearsome creeps
on the subway and don't blink
I drive 10½ mph average
on my way to work.

I beep swerve
can make a 3 lane street
4 or even 5 lanes

I'm a New Yorker now
can hail a cab
carry many keys
and little cash
few credit cards
walk tough
spread my valuables
about my body
wear low heels
sneakers with my suits
wait on line not in line
with great patience
(I never knew I had
such patience)

Jane Navarre

I let my bank take
5 working days to clear
a cashier's check
and never murmur

I doubled my salary
1/3'ed my life style
I'm a New Yorker now.
I saw Paul Newman on the street.

I o.d. on possibility.
For entertainment I can go to
the opera, the theatre, a lecture
museums shops restaurants
neighborhoods bars clubs games
such riches
no human could possibly
do it all
I'm a New Yorker now
stay behind locked doors
watch tv, think about it

Jane Navarre

Laurie Swyers

Hummingbird

You brought me,
cupped in your hand
the questions of children
lifeless and hard
a hummingbird found
by my door

whose beak
soft and curved to
milk the rose
now preserved in your wonder,
had caught me watching
the same question a week before
but too quick to decipher
flew from thought.

I have soared horizontal
beyond this flesh
tiny hellicopters
in the sun,
Oh you king,
architect
in my palm.

PLACE

Michael Blair

from *The Ice Cream Man*

The Drive   There

        the road itself is called
    The Grand Army of the Republic Highway
       or the Anthony Wayne Trail
carved out by zealous Virginians and Pennsylvanians
uprooting trees in their eagerness to catch Tecumseh —
it is called Wayne's Trace from Fort Wayne to Detroit

      this is part of the Old Hull Road
which the retreating General took through what
   was then called the Great Black Swamp —
                      now called Toledo

the great, and wise Pontiac himself
moved his lodges and his warriors down here
   after raising the seige of Detroit in '63
but mostly I call it West or East bound two four
come on   forget history
                    the drive
    is the same coming and going   anytime
I always got my squawker on   but headed West
I almost never turn the talker on   I can't
 too many breaker-breakers and good buddies —
but   since I usually got my eight-track cookin
if I call at all ya got one West-bound Tape-Player
   lookin   for that clean shot at Defiance-town o.k.?
     ya got the lowdown Brown?

There is Springtime on the river
here   a house new since last year
there   the bank cut down around that canal lock

      this has always been a professional road
   this path by the Maumee
Red   White men   runaway slaves mule
skinners humiliated Generals
                 and Mad ones
        downright pissed-off at the government
           Bonus Marchers eighteen wheelers
               all of us
                  keepin our eyes and our ears on
                     lookin for Bear

Bond Street, Napoleon

When the sun shines on my truck
  it hurts my eyes to lean outside
  so I lean way back on the freezer
the very tops of Diane's breasts
sneek peeks at me in the rear-view

And I really thought
  she didn't know I was peeking
  until she bought the yellow halter
"Do you like it?" laughing
  "I bought it for you"

        for a season or two
   til she's sixteen at least
  forgetting her bra
  and Laughing that laugh that
  pointed chin is worth a drumstick
     a day to me

Ice Cream Man
(a turn of seasons)

      I guess I never
saw it as a money making proposition
        I just drive

Constant avocation
   longer than my marriage
undemanding
            as a Summer day
I don't know why I do it
things sort of work into place

      the winter melts
    children dream of Summer
     and I bring it closer
I am the King of May
 for seven years now

      little girls all grow up
  twelve is now nineteen
and what the moms and daddies bought
        the boyfriends buy

even jaded twenty-threes
   still get it free sometimes
a Summer day
          a flirting girl
    blowing hot and cold
  another ice cream season
  headed down the road

Michael Blair

Hey Mister
Hey YOU
HEY ICE CREAM MAN

gimme sum'nfree
        cause yer my friend
        cause I'm yer pal
        because you're nice
        cause it's my birthday
          it's my brother's birthday
my baby sister doesn't know what money is

  gimme sum'n to take my sister
she broke her leg and lost her money
    I'll pay you tomorrow
        next time
        next week
      as soon as I get my allowance
      as soon as my mom gets home
         my dad
      as soon as my brother unlocks the sitter
            she's in the bathroom
            in the shower
            the basement
      it really IS my birthday today

my mom said you could give it to us today
  cause we don't got no money
            be nice
        be a pal
      be cool
   c'mon slick   be hip
        don't be hard
        chump
        you dick
          you're bogue

Michael Blair

>   I don't like you anymore
>   I'm not gonna buy anything from you
>   even when I do get money
>   and none of my friends will, either
>   c'mon
>   you're hard
>   it's too hot
>   it's only ice cream
>   my brother SAID this was money!

a late night run from Defiance

        one
        two red joints
        I have this vision —

            someone else's rearview . . .
        ice cream truck on end
        over end down the highway

        side-swiped by a drunken kid
        on his way to Napoleon
        bleary eyes staring wide
                        on red

                  over at mine
        glued into his mirror
        picture of a white truck
                    bursting

        into a blossom of Bomb
        pops and screwballs —
            scatterring rte. 24
                with free ice cream
                for miles around . . .

Michael Blair

Coming Home
("Haven't you out-grown that job yet?")

    Now that I'm stuck in traffic
      East of Napoleon what I should have
        told you isn't enough or what
  I should have done doesn't tell me
    what in Hell I should be doing?

maybe it's the brittle moon
    in splinters on the river
or the freight train progression
of betrayals my life is becoming
  that has rewarded me with this:
      Ice Cream Mythos
    sometimes freezer burn a
     couple of poems

          I could be back at the factory
          I could be married again
          I could be a Father

I've been silent some nights
and don't smoke cigarettes for sixty miles
I told myself I'd do it often
    I'd do it always until tonight
  in the full moon of October
I was East-bound the last time
in an Ice Cream truck.

Michael Blair

the ice cream man

the ice cream man: one of many, driven, restless, seeing, constant.
the true ice cream man: at peace, works with speed, maintains relationships with many, is well supplied, drives carefully.
the true ice cream man: works with joy, works for pleasure, draws out all from within, brings delight, remembers the desires of others, drives each street just once.
the carrion ice cream man: works with purpose, is reckless, carries a limited menu; lies to children with a straight face, is a thief, works for money, drives the same streets over and over.

— Traditional
(native to inhabitants of Trilby)

Bob Phillips

Hiroshima Memorial Barbecue

you might have been frying
a chunk of baloney
on a backyard grill
in Toledo, Ohio,
1960-something.
your wife stares with scorn
at the sizzling piece of labonza
that you insisted on buying
at the amazing sale price
of 39¢ a pound.
who could pass it up?
and there you are,
searing that lovely tube of hoof-meat,
when the fatal acorn drops.
suddenly,
something is terribly wrong in your backyard.
the sky lights up as if there'd been a miracle.
Detroit, Michigan whips past your ears
in a sheet of hot vapor.
your wife is suddenly overwhelmed
with a desire to hold you.
if there is any last thought at all
passing thru your brain for an instant,
perhaps you recall
sneaking into your child's room
to sleep there
on a lonely night.
perhaps your last thought
is full of hopeless anger,
your heart breaking,
your love aching,
the spatula in your left hand melting.

Sanctuary

inside of me,
as if in my chest,
there is what seems to be a lake.
it is a small lake,
but it is deep and clear and black.
around this lake are bright green lily pads,
reeds,
& tender shoots of summer trees.
there are ducks & fish,
the red-winged blackbird,
insects,
frogs & turtles.
on the lake's surface
is a small red boat with oars.
something is in the boat.
it is my heart.

Red Rowboat Blues

you first realize it when you're 2 yrs. old:
there is no place to go
that is not up, down, or crazy.

you grow older,
perhaps 30,
& take up fishing for your mental health.

sitting in a red rowboat,
all alone,
the sun goes down.

the reeds in the dusk are ecstasy.

Bob Phillips

Rayon Shirt Item

I throw a stick into the woods
for the dog to chase—
it brings back not the stick
but something from a bush
by the edge of the trees—
it is a rayon shirt w/tag.
I say, "good dog."
it wags its tail.
I walk into the house.

the next day, I write home to mom:
"hey mom, the dog fetched me a rayon shirt
from the field out back. it's got a tag from Pennys."

a week later I receive a letter from mom:
"a cheap rayon shirt from Penny's, you goddamn fool!
why couldn't that stupid dog fetch you
a nice flannel shirt from Sears? made in Taiwan?
give that jerk ass dog of yours a kick in the heinie for me.
love, mom."

the next day, I go out to the yard
and beat the dog to death
with an old piece of plumbers pipe—
then I hang it by the neck in the cherry tree—
with the rayon shirt—
then I go out in the cornfield
and take a leak.

Bob Phillips

Miracle Fabric

don't bleach that rayon, buddy
it'll wreck your shirt
now you see it now you don't
back to Pennys, back to Sears
& K-Mart

what was that flag made of?
the one that they wired on the moon?
one big step for man?
hell, that weren't no step, buddy
that was the rayon boogie shuffle
don't you watch T.V.?
it's the latest dance
don't you know all about miracle fabrics
& which detergent to use?

meanwhile, back on the moon
after everyone's gone
a herd of lunar penguins
gather about a polyester flag —
one penguin says to another, "rayon shirt"
the other one says, "yeh, moon feathers"
a third penguin says, "moon rocks"
another one says, "yeh, they keep stealing our washing
    machines"
they all gallop away like slow-motion beachballs
knowing how to have a good laugh
like all good penguins do,
"wok! wok! wok! wok! wok! wok! wok!"

Bob Phillips

Western Beauty

in the American Heritage Dictionary of the English
    Language
there is a picture of a girl.
she is the little picture at the edge of the page
that shows you the word.
the girl in this picture is of the word, "lava-lava."
it is a kiltlike garment of cotton print worn by Polynesians,
especially Samoans.
the girl in this picture has a lithe lean body.
she wears orchids in her hair.
she is beautiful.
the lava-lava she is wearing would come off
with the tug of a finger.
studying the American Heritage Dictionary
I am falling in love.
resisting the urge to masturbate, I notice her brassiere.
something is wrong.
it looks manufactured & she shouldn't be wearing one.
it is because this is the American Heritage Dictionary.
then I notice her face.
something is terribly wrong here, too.
she has rounded features.
she looks exactly like Soupy Sales!
I think: if she were the girl next door
she would be, "the ugly chick with the fantastic body."
jokes would be made about putting a grocery bag on her
    head.
this is too much for me to bear.
then I realize she would also be called "nigger"
or "chink" or "spic" or "flip."
studying the American Heritage Dictionary is a sad lesson
in love, democracy and beauty.
but this poem I enjoy as a kind of scholarship.

Mysterious Laundry Haiku

you wash it out
hang it out on the line to dry
& your neighbors
instead of looking at it
avert their eyes
they've been to the laundromat enough times
they're ready to sell out and buy a dryer
or pick up a rock
& beat the shit out of a rayon shirt

Testing out the Neighborhood

if the family pet makes it,
chances are,
your kids will make it, too.
and if your pet, such as a kitty,
disappears completely,
or is discovered a week later,
a few streets over,
flat as paper,
take heart!
neighborhoods don't really count.
traffic is everywhere.
this earth is blessed
with an abundance of life
as well as death.
chances are,
your kids will be okay.

Bob Phillips

Zona Gale

Greening

come March
I am persimmon
when full buds
burst
and everything greens again
fruit nubs erupting
leaves unfolding

I stand
tall, slim, straight
copious numbers
in the dark wood
born in fertile loam
from seeds water carried
or animal dropped, roots
tentacled deep
rain and sun raised me
wind sang and stripped me

wild
growing free
I bear
sweet fall fruit

Metamorphosis

come May
wrapped in a cocoon
snug in the fork of a tree
quiet, dark, dreamless
time drifts

my cells groan, snap—
I emerge
light as fluff
glorious, silent

I move through air
with the windsong
cradled in the sepals of flowers
delicately moving
harmless
without fear
sometimes
a blossom hides me

July Harvest

currants
sun ripe
sour
from the low green bush
by our back porch
burst in the kettle

strain
steam
bubble
long wood spoon stirs
sugar sweetens
mass thickens

into clear glass cups
to cool
ruby red
I love
to make currant jelly
eat freshly made
thick on buttered bread

Winston Smith

Flashback

Interstate
75
rides the heaped up hogback
of earth, strides
across the old south city
and dams the thwarted streets
where I look down to see . . .

Time
leaching from red bricks
of old buildings
staining the ambient air
along a stagnant street
with mezzotints
of sun and shade.

Queer quirk
to trigger so uncalled
this vivid flash
from buried deep
in twists and turns
of me.

Riffling through
the layered years
to an early page
where walking
I should meet
myself again
on a younger street.

River Morning Vignette

Fog fades upstream blurring yet
all sharp edges
still waters by the docks forget
ways past marshy sedges.

On a river with no wind
floating
fallen yellow leaves suspend
on a placid nothingness.

Invert images amaze
where
birds reflect their flapping ways
upon a startled river.

Seagulls crowd, a foamdrift spun
of settling wings
on a mudbank where the sun
strikes early.

One white heron stilted stands
alone in shallows
silent stalker of the sands
for the fated minnows.

From dark river depths below
a drowning moon
wavers in the sinking glow
of night undone.

The Wind

I never saw the wind, but still
I met it one day on a hill
A little wind come frolicking
an innocent and artless thing
tossing flowers as it came
alone, attendant on its game.

I never saw the wind, but yet
on a hillside one day we met
a little wind without a care
that came on me all unaware
and paused a bit to gently place
cool curious fingers on my face.

They say the wind's invisible
but yet one day upon a hill
a little wind and I did meet
It came and went on lightsome feet
and up the hill where it did pass
left waving footprints in the grass.

Winston Smith

Herbert Scott

from *The Shoplifter's Handbook*

Directions

Choose a fat goose store stuffed with customers.
Keep your head on straight, let your eyes
be rovers. Indecision breeds suspicion.
If you know where you are going get there.

Meat puts muscle on your frame.
Endow yourself if God didn't.
A cod piece for your crotch,
a brace of filets for your chest.

Slip oysters in your pockets but not sardines.
A broken arm slings a chicken.
Fold the *News* around a steak.

Remember, good things come in small packages.
Cigarettes go up in smoke,
eye shadows disappear in purses,
pills and purges leave no trace.

Precautions

Take only what you can conceal.
It's a free country. You may return
an empty bottle, fill up again,
become a regular customer.

Carry no identification, labels, fingerprints,
pictures of loved ones, birthmarks.
Forget your name. Remember your sex.
If you become confused
touch yourself gently between the legs.

If you get caught choose
a new name to plead your case:
Amanda, worthy to be loved, Manfred,
peace among men. Later you may need
Delores of sorrows, Hector holding fast.

Guilt

The time will come
you will grow a hand on your shoulder
walk with a limp surprise yourself
in the mirror. Disguise. Dye hair.
Fake a moth of a moustache feeding
beneath your nose. You think
it's real until it flies away.

You have a pocketful of moths, of holes,
your clothes are full of openings.
You fear that everything will show,

will come alive, chickens wing
from your arms, your body leak,
soft goods rise like kites
to string you from the ceiling.

Confession wags your tongue. Clip its tail.
Suddenly you want purity and nakedness.
Give to charity what you can't use or sell.
Store up credit and good will. Begin again.

Accessories

Your children grow hands like empty
    plates.
Hold them upside down, they sprout
a possum pouch. Lick their snouts
until they learn to smell each other
out. Do not give them names.

Let their teachers try to pry them open.
They remain closed as apples.
Take a bite. Their eyes and mouths are
    white.
They're solid. Chew into the seeds
you'll spit them out.

Leave them in their skins, you nurtured
    them.
There's nothing you can do
to change the way their fingers grow.

Warning

Trust no one. You have no friends.
Your appetite empties pockets, the cost
of living balloons from your breath.
Can you walk a straight line?
No one will pass this test.

Alibis

I am your long lost son, your daughter,
Don't you remember me, Father?
My sister's sick mother's giving birth
a catastrophe fell off the shelf into my shirt.
It's the first time I forgot to pay.
They made me do it, my starving children,
my lame dog, my drunken father
who beats me with a hose,
I want to see a priest, my dead mother,
the President. Please forgive me. Forgive me.

Susan Dwyer

Ungers' Ice Cream Store

To Ungers'
We went
With pennies
Dreams
And hungers

Visions of
Enough
And buddies
Boasting
Baby-sitting funds

Tongued
Cool scoops
Swallowed slurps
Burped hot fudge
And guzzled fizz

Then
Slaked
But craving
Turned to
Double Bubble

Popped
Two-deckers
From cold puckers
Mustached
With pistachio

Tested two-bit yo-yos
On stuck fingers
Lingered
Over Superman
And wallowed home

Still
Wanting

Richard K. Morgenstern

Pump in a Field

Alone, rusting,
    base crumbling
        and overgrown,
arm raised,
    awaiting the onslaught
        of perspiring children
fresh from the mow
    and fighting to be first,
        it stands ready

There, in the silence,
    broken only by
        an occasional caw
and the swish
    of soft winds,
        moving through grain
in a field still working
    and earning its keep,
        it waits

Arnold J. Koester

Just a Boy from Berkey

I'm just a boy from Berkey
Humble and solitary
Beginnings from a flat farming land

I'm just a boy from Berkey
When life gets complicated
I live as simply as I can

I'm just a boy from Berkey
I didn't have much to do
Got my thrills from fertile fantasy

I'm just a boy from Berkey
And this is my vocation
To turn manure dreams to reality

I'm just a boy from Berkey
Population maybe five-hundred
And that's to include
Cows, pigs, and chickens

I'm just a boy from Berkey
A one-stoplight town
The first one in Ohio
And they hung it upside down

I'm just a boy from Berkey
Growing up with tomatoes
The fruit of migrant labor
To the promised land from Mexico

I'm just a boy from Berkey
I didn't travel all that far
Except through science fiction
Space trekking to the stars

I'm just a boy from Berkey
Got high by climbing trees
Wooden arms rocked me gently in the breeze

I'm just a boy from Berkey
Private and quiet
Nightly serenaded by the crickets

Arnold J. Koester

Joe Sheffler

Manual For A 3-Day Mountain Walk

The Central Mountains

The Central Mountain Range is the composite name of four mountain systems the largest of which is Chungyang Shan which means "Central Mountain." Its highest peaks are Nanhuta Shane (12,454ft), Chilai Shan (11,624), and Kwan Shan (12,185). These peaks form the main water divide for the island of Taiwan, tilting the rivers west into the Formosa Strait, or east into the Pacific.

In geologic time, thrust-faulting lifted nearly all of eastern Taiwan creating a spine which almost precisely divides the land mass into halves. The range extends 168 miles north to south and from 10 to 35 miles from east to west. Its boundaries are two steep cliffs: a fault line separating the mountains from the alluvial plains to the west, and a fault scarp stopping the mountains on the east at a thin rift valley and the sea.

The make up of the Central Mountains is old rock schist and gneiss: limestone, sandstone, slate and shale. The geology is gigantic faulting and folding with strong, continual erosion caused by extremely heavy rain fall, up to 160 inches annually in some places. Long and persistent erosion has worn these mountains into a large number of peaks, 30 of them over 10,000 feet. Relief between peaks is rarely more than 1000 feet which gives the entire range a plateau-like appearance with steep, pure river valleys and precipitous canyons cutting into a mountainside ribboned by many waterfalls.

The Central Mountains are deep green, thick forested and nearly impenetrable. The flora is extremely various and beautiful ranging from dense undergrowth jungle-like tree-fern and palm in the lower valleys, to large camphor, oak, maple and chestnut on the middle slopes. Nearer the crests are giant hemlock and juniper trees and areas of Alpine meadow.

The peoples of these mountains are of a distinctive aboriginal habit and language, theoretically of Malay-Polynesian origin. They are clear-eyed, intense, and known to love dancing.

The walk described in this manual proceeds 3 days from Lushan to the southeast, along power station trails, over Chilai Shan — the heart of the Central Mountains — and down to the coastal city of Hualien on the Pacific.

Application Form for Permit for Alien Entering Aboriginal Area

You need a *Mountain Pass*:

A Chinese name
A sex
A nationality
A passport
A position
A duration
An object
An area
Enclosed documents
Remarks
2 photos
A signature
A date

To get into the Mountains

Joe Sheffler

Go Light

A canvas back pack
a cup
hiking shoes
several pair of thick socks
one long one short sleeve shirt
shorts poncho knife tape
rubbing alcohol Ritalin Reds
dried fruit peanuts candy
you're ready

Plans

for Zoe Zapotosky

Taichung by 10:30 train
Taxi 2 hours up to Wusheh
Wake the Priest
Get maps and Names of Stations
Breakfast: bread & sweet bean curd soup
8:40 bus to Lushan
Hike forty-five hundred feet to Tien Chih
At 10,000 rest for the night
For the Full Moon Festival
Way up there

The Power Stations

                      Tien Chih
                      (2860)

            Yun Hai   Kuai Lin
            (2340)   (2109)

       Tun Yuan   Chi Lai
       (1751)   (1126)

     Lushan   Pan Shih
     (1391)   (1048)

  Wusheh   Shui Lien
  (1148)   (385)

                              Tung Men
                              (165)

1 meter = 3.28 feet

Joe Sheffler

Manual for Poisonous Snakes

for Dick Sawyer

Banded Krait, Umbrella Snake, 100 Segment Snake
nocturnal, near water
docile but known to bite
neurotoxic one/fifth mortality

*

Naja Naja, Chinese Cobra, Spectacle Cobra
aggressive and moody
flaired hood and soft hiss
above the break
nerve toxic and deadly

*

Russell's Viper, Seven Pacer, Chain Snake
nervous and vicious
strikes without notice
excited the body vibrates
a low rasping of scales and gutteral hiss
neurotoxic *and* hemotoxic
high mortality

*

Acutus, 100 Pacer, Five Pacer, Snake of 100 Designs
coiled always and ready
to deliver with large hinged fangs
quantities of hemotoxic high
mortality by all indigenous people
well respected and recognized most
venomous of snakes

*

Bamboo Viper, Bamboo Snake, Red-Tail Snake
arboreal & active at night
hangs by a prehensile-like tail
vibrates its warning blood toxic
but not greatly feared

*

Habu, Turtle-Design Snake
in the grass or in caves full or city
one even taken from a western-style house!
hassled it strikes quick unpredictable
with well developed fangs
blood toxic moderate mortality

Bus Ride

There is the smell of animals
men and women
mixed in the morning air there
is an open cunt on the pantyless girl
across the aisle a student's hands
citied and out of place there
is a boy with bad teeth and
probably in pain
pushing a wet rag in his mouth
in his hand there is a copy of Russell's philosophy
translated there is
the chatter of mountain language
and roar of ancient mercedes
sacks of weird vegetables
straw baskets of bricks
bundles and ways to carry them
the dark men and women who do
and there is a difference here
of way and use

Joe Sheffler

K. Enters the Mountains

Uncertainty at first
provincial police scrutinize your maps
unintelligible but why did they think
you were here where all strangers enter
the mountains regardless of race
here and there a face but no intention in it
out finally on a *guess* and brown grass
to where the trail splits up country
and you can see your way
and a Spectacle Cobra coils out of it
yet in the first hour and already
wild and beautiful as hell

Naming and Saying

Names come from plants and animals
in the mountains

Plain of Rattan and
Lake of Rattan

Valley of Deer and
Hill where the Deer are Plentiful

Emminent Monkey

In the old language wild animals were numerous
and vegetation flourished

Joe Sheffler

Journey to Yun Hai

Stopped to eat in the rain
somehow missing the station
aching in the middle of the trail we sat
and cheered ourselves with apples
and logic:

Having passed the station
we were nearer to the next
optimistic of its place
in reference to our own:

Where it is a cold hard rain
contains us and our spirits
hard to maintain we are anywhere
in reference:

Suddenly a brown fact of cabin
and place from the rain
contains the crazy man we'd heard of
talk pussy and booze
brings o-soba in big bowls to warm us
wants us to stay for the night
warns us away from the Mountain
from the climb after dark
too dangerous to pursue:

You might ask is this a *real* man
or am I making him up

Joe Sheffler

Walking

The way up
is calves and heels
stretching the small back

And the way down
is toes and ankles
arching the torso back

the same way

Up From Twilight

From twilight up
and light changing and changing
Then night
    like a bat
    like a shale path
Breathless over the edge
    like a loose stone
    like a weak bridge
Waiting

Supper at Tien Chih

Eating with my fingers
    curried mountain quail
    killed with a cruel long barreled gun:
    At night
    A bright light on his forehead
    blinding them
    blowing them to bits
Placing their fine bones by my bowl

Noon at Kuai Lin

Finding the cabin abandoned
I poke in its stores
cabbage and onions
peanuts and dried pork
potatoes and greens
dried fish and rice
all kept in the clean kitchen
located off the central room
and left of a corridor with many rooms
right of the sunlit room
I rested in
on clean *tatame* mats
to the soft pluck of a pendulum
I dreamed then
of lying in a sunlit room in the mountains
resting from a long walk

Joe Sheffler

Strangeness at Chi Lai

Halfway to the next station
I pass the work crew cutting the trail
quiet faced men who look through me
who catch up in the rain
and lead me down quickly to the cabin
fixing hot tea
my bath and bed for the night
then sit with the lights on
looking down over me and laughing loudly
unnerving me
so I can't get to sleep

Cedar Satori

for Robinson Jeffers

As far as you come
up under moss and fern covered
cedar is rain-colored green mud
and a soil smell of rainforest molts
its oldest tree inward from man
and many bridges high above water
bouncing as you walk over
around gorges a thousand feet deep
valleys alternately seen and not seen
gauzed distances and rain and
jungle grass Habu Cobra and Krait
enough venom and places to get lost
tired traveller you are finally quiet
as moss on rainforest cedar
quiet as rainforest itself everywhere
quiet as the awesome stone
loneliness of mountains

Over East

From Chilai
a chalky cliff cuts diagonally
up the mountain each bend
seems an end hiking up
over washouts and thin ledge
squeezed to string precipitous
the great mountain behind
where you walked yesterday
is shale and slick coming down
the divide eastward through rainforest
and tall grass all the way
to Hualien and the sea

Coda/ Coming Down

The power station
is a quiet afternoon courtyard
I walk into startled
by a saggy-titted cur
looting the kitchen

Below is the river deep translucence
of green gyre and roar
down steep drop
into wide alluvial fan
rice paddies
bamboo and banana trees
Ocean

Behind is sun set
and Mountains
the thin trail through

Joe Sheffler

Tom Barden

Cold hard money

cold hard money runs this town
but even the spark plug trucks
slide in the snow today
no Cadillacs roll
out of motor city in this stuff
and everybody's in the tavern
after work

Molly rolls her glass
in her jangled hands
and plays with the
stack of coins on the counter
it could be Paris
or East Village
the way the talk runs
books and music

Molly's got a man at home
she says
but he'll have to feed
his own
fucking cat
her eyes
have given up

it doesn't matter
what he does
she says
she just can't feel him
it doesn't matter
if it rains
her heart is dry
if it snows
her heart is drifting

Shorty Greenberg's
Russian Turkish Steam Bath

I walk up and down
in front of six old men
with their heads bent down in their hands
the bodies are slabbed out in tiers
around the furnace
a bucket of water runs over slowly
water to spare
the silence is cordial
the talk curt

more steam?
why not

I pick up the bucket
walk toward the door
water sloshes against my balls
and the velvet black smoked pipes
it beads and dances

here goes

from the top tier
an old man stands up in
a torrent of words

wait a goddamn minute   let me offa here
why you gotta fuck with it anyhow

he wades through the young men
dripping the sweat of last night's whiskey

I let fly
steam spits back in a pipe-break
blow-up, fist unclenching sigh

I stretch out flat on the sweet wood bench
the old men turn over   the young men turn over
water trickles   silence
my head bends down in my hands

the old men leave in a trickle
out into the snow
home to their Saturday women
all droozy and clear   their balls all tight
the last one tells us this elaborate story
walking up and down

toledo poem

*since you passed here yesterday
we have sold seven mobile homes*
—*billboard sign in toledo*

I

the sky
is stitched
with birds
as I step out on the frozen breakers
of Lake Erie
exploring past the last footprints
walking to Canada
I think of Jolliet in 1669
paddling over the St. Clair
paddling down the Detroit
until his eyes opened
full of maps
on this
I poke the iceribs

think of the fish below
their surprise to hear me
tapping across their ceiling
there is a photo of the governor
on my folding map
he looks puzzled in his tie
he says
industry, business, welcome
I imagine him standing on the hillside
at Kent State
his arms outstretched
chanting industry business welcome

I fold him
back in my pocket
and look around
that shoreline is Ohio
to the left is Michigan
all Indian names
and all trapped
like the lakes, locked
look they freeze entirely over
you can jump on them
they say there is oil
under the soil under the fish
derricks will rise
out of these waters
jungle jims nobody plays on
signs— do not walk on this lake
shit, I wanted a sea
this is the edge of America too
the third coast
and it's just a lake
by a swamp
the water I live by
and do not understand
except you take Route 2, east
look for seagulls
and go home

II

So, maybe you can tell me
if I say, baby
I like your company
where I can find this place
get me high
drive me around
tell me you own the town
the street names are your ancestors
there are factory strikes
and spark plug fortunes
at your family reunion
so maybe you can show me
how to live here
take me to a premiere
of the symphony
good movies
good jazz
where you go
what you do
I'll show you my sheets
my hot confusion
my dreams
in the huge pavillion
in the Wildwood Preserve
where the city fathers
will never find us
please baby
I need to know
make a strong case for here
for anywhere
for terrorism
Zionism
resistance
plain living
repose
tell me your dreams
what you would name the streets

if they really were yours
what you would name me if I were
what kind of street would I be
for you
why don't you have any secrets
what will your body mean to me later
what noise do you suppose the river makes
when the ice breaks up
and sends forty-ton blocks
crashing into the startled lake
in the spring

III

what is that seagull going in the metropark
he seems so out of place
whitecap white among the maples
he looks like a senior citizen
in a government van
but he seems to make himself at home
he chips at straws he
hops across the bike trail
he picks at tree seeds
scratches
all untidy and unconcerned
he's seen the rolling ocean
been
stitched into the sky
he looks up
and hops into the air
of toledo
he doesn't care where he lives

A Duck May Be Somebody's Mother

Be kind to your friends in the swamp
   of their own aspirations
   following their genius
   trying to be of good cheer
Be kind to yourself there next to them
   and to your feet below
   take off your socks in the afternoon
   of your efforts and air them out
Be kind to your fellows in the food chain
   remember, if you lose regret
   when you mash a frog with those Michelins
   you have lost too much
   be kind to your kidneys, get out and walk
Be kind to your heart, it wants a good conversation
   chances are you have begun to ignore it
   because it has begun to talk nonsense
   become a mystic
   this is especially so if you are in your thirties
Be kind to your thirties, they are the peak
   and kind to nonsense
   and pity the poor scientist
   intent on the truth
Be kind to the truth, it's stranger than fiction

Be kind to all fools (even the one in the mirror)

Be kind to some piece of geography
   pull shopping carts out of the creek
   give up cutting some piece of lawn
   it will give back to prairie
   this will be kind to your neighbors
   giving them topics for gossip
   also, they will be reintroduced to wildflowers
Be kind to wildflowers, to columbine to chickory
   to the majestic Queen Anne's lace

Be kind to your dreams
   they are your only world without money
   fill them with wildflowers, with trillium and clover
   fireweed and yellowrocket
   this will be kind to the unseen bees in your dreamfields

Be kind to God's dream called nature
   the mink and the heron the groundhog and the deer
   to all lifeforms, except maybe ticks and fleabeetles
Be kind to God by the care of Her creatures
   even the ones at typewriters, mirrors
   at work at rest at wit's end   who else?   be kind to

Bob Tomanski

At Home

I feel fat
    as the moon
tonight:
        round
           white
  & pockmarked.
No
    argument
this belly holds
    too much beer;
who can find a man's
    shortcomings
when he spends his time
    gratefully at home?
Plenty
    to read,
and free
      iris
from a
    neighbor's yard.

LOVE

Peggie Cypher

Pet Therapy I

he gave the young woman
a kiss

Pet Therapy II

he gave the old woman
a puppy

George de Chant

7 fantasies

1

we are in a cottage
in southern indiana
we're living off your
ex-ol'man,
infact this is his cottage
that you got in the settlement
we've been here since spring
we know of three amish
restaurants that serve good
food and are inexpensive
for the last two months
all we do is swim to
the raft and lay out
and you know your tan lines
cut through my trunks
like an audubon
bird call
i'm writing you love poems
on your back
in the karma sutra oil
that your ex
gave you when he was
trying to get back

2

i'm married to poetry
i read and write poetry
all during the day
i eat poetry

(and when it gets
back to $40 an ounce)
i smoke poetry
poetry is my security
but
at night you are my
mistress
you are the fury of
the night
of my life
that sometimes
makes even the most
beautiful poem
tedious
we are happy but
sometimes the angst
gets the better of us
and we have ballroom
fights
we call each other names
til both of us are crying
then we make love

    3

we are walking down the street
and people stare at us
like tourists
because together
we are
a beautiful land
that people want
to book tours to

    4

you are ann
and i am gary
a couple that
i work with

you come to work
and confide in the
mopper how happy
you are
how i just bought
you pearl earrings
for our 3rd month
anniversary
we have corny nick
names for each other
and when i pick
you up for a date
i let you put the
radio on the country
western station i
can't stand

        5

i am a general in a war
that is to end
all police actions
i am a god to my men
we are preparing
for a big attack
that will change
the course of this war
the men are nervous
but trust my decisions
they think i'm invincible
because during an earlier
battle i walked onto the
beach amidst an aerial attack
with bombs exploding all
around and was not hit
so my men are ready to
follow me into war

(which shows how
ludicrous war is
when soldiers
follow a man with a
death wish)
the reason i walked on
the beach is because
i think you sent me
a "dear john letter"
that was really sent
by your drunken step-father
who is trying to
seduce you

    6

i am a critic
writing an essay
on your beauty
but at the same time
i come spinning
towards you
stalking in
the literary
circles of a seafox

    7

you are a waitress in a bar
that i go to on thursday
and i am pathetically
infatuated with you
worst of all i am apt
to say stupid things like
"if you don't have pitted
prunes then could i have
a date
with you?"

which luckily for me
you seem to think is cute
you won't go out with me
because you have a boyfriend
but then for some unexplained
reason
like in a greek play
zeus comes down with a thunder
bolt and your boyfriend is gone
and when the dry ice vapor fades
you and i are lying on
a king size waterbed

    curtain

Barbara Claire Kasselmann

panther
in spring

through the warm may night
i drive
two hundred miles

from the valley
your voice
calls

spring's second half moon
ringed by mauve

breasts cry
body swells

in the pale blue
dawn

i touch my tongue
to your soft damp
skin

the day we hiked up abrams creek

dark waxy laurel
crawled
and climbed
all about us

carolina july
steamy
hot

golden earrings
sweat-stained t-shirts
and soft damp silk
fell

as warm moist mother
earth absorbed you
and me

mockingbirds
and white water
scarcely breathed

after we had gone
black bears would come
in the night
to worship

Barbara Claire Kasselmann

shower

soaping my breasts
from behind
always did excite you

especially in the early morning
when the cold december sun
lurked yet below the horizon

and there was still time
to miss the bus

thursday night
at the great
harvest moon celebration

thick moon
full, fleshy
papaya-colored

pouring its seeds
into a dark
river

your long fingers
gliding
through soft gold down

that covers the outer curves
of my
thighs

Barbara Claire Kasselmann

lunch at the lily

i remember you as eyes
that saw
as hands and skin
that were touch
as tongue
that knew every flavor
and pleasure

when i see you stare
beyond me

tasting not
the words you eat

leaving half the wine
in the bottom
of your glass

i can scarcely recall
your name

Barbara Claire Kasselmann

reunion

you flew a thousand miles
to love me
for one more night

amid piles of soft white satin
i fed you
olives by candelight

you wove my hair
into long dark braids
like before

we drank pinot noir
and laughed about the part
that fell off the car on vancouver island
in '76

at dawn
we sipped black coffee
from styrofoam cups
at the end of the airport

as i turned to watch the snow
drift back across the runway
i wondered if you
really had been here
at all

moving into winter

forty-six times
i have watched
the seasons turn
in this direction

there will not be
forty-six more times
for me

locust bean pods
lie crinkled and dark
upon the ground

birds
no longer sing
on heavy pear branches

fewer hours
to gather my children
about me

less time to fill
empty pages
with rich words

precious long sundays
to lie with my skin
against the skin
of my young
lover

Barbara Claire Kasselmann

Donna Rowe

The Power of Love

    I am the queen of loneliness
   the goddess of emptiness
The princess of nothingness
  and the Empress of sadness

Come save me my love
  From the depths of dark despair
Fill my senses with the fragrance of love
  the touch of love
  the sound & sight of love
and let me taste your love.

You will make me the queen of happiness
  the Goddess of faithfulness
The princess of peacefulness
  And the Empress of Blissfulness

      Come Rescue Me

Sandy Smith

Poem

Mr Death
oh so handsome
with soft curly dark hair and Clark Gable moustache,
stood
nose to nose,
chest to small bosom,
stomach to stomach,
thigh to thigh
business shoe to moccasin,
and tried to seduce me
with his laughing blue/grey eyes.
He grinned,
I smiled.
He asked,
I answered.
Then
with his shit-ass grin
he opened his mouth
 - that sensuous mouth -
and swallowed me whole.

Jane Johanson

from *Loving, Leaving and Living Again*

The Novelette

Waiting for a train at Saint Lazare,
Too young to travel, too young by far
To pick a novelette from the stand,
And yet I do!

The train to Louveciennes is red,
And as it moves, I see
The lurid pictures shake and quake,
Naked women with long hair,
Black stockings gartered at the thigh.
I am too young to read the words.
And yet I do!

They tell
of boots, whips, alcoves and peepholes,
Frilled panties, suppers at midnight,
Things I am too young to know.
And yet I do!

I am at home, hiding my novelette
Among the books all leather-bound and proud,
A street urchin among the dons.
This is what I seem today:
A woman of the streets.
I should not feel that way,
And yet I do!

The Rift

Just yesterday
you found my nipples pink and tight,
my body comforting,
loved the softness of my skin.
My lips alive with kisses
gave the pleasures that you sought.
You whispered your delight.
Today your voice is soundless
like a song already ended
and the rift cannot be mended.

The Letter

That first fear of loss,
that first foreboding,
was in me, long before
the letter came.
Stark and understated
its message scorched my flesh.
My world lay dead
wrapped in a winding sheet
that bore his words,
once written down so neat
in his fine hand,
now writ large, filling every room
like radiation, bringing death.
They penetrated deep,
turned me to stone,
and I was crated Trans-Atlantic home,
none to grieve my grieving.
Grieve for a stone
sans eyes to see, sans lips to speak?
And graven on the stone, the words
"He loves you not."

Winter Set

Put the walking shoes away.
We shall nevermore together
walk along our favorite way
scale the banks or wade the streams,
not again except in dreams.

Put away the summer tent.
Summer will not come again.
Was this really your intent
that we'd never sleep together
in the woods or by the streams
not again except in dreams?

Put away the gloves and skis
even if the snow is deepening.
We shall never chase each other
down the slopes, nor be together
near the glowing winter's fire.
Never can we so aspire.

Now your voice seems strangely cold
and your blue eyes glint as ice
and your words are few and cutting
like a bitter winter's wind.
I must go to bed so lonely
without comfort, without cover, without lover.

Jane Johanson

The Request

Write it all down, my love,
for my past hovers over the present
and my voice is uncertain.
I speak with laughter in my eyes
but my words weep.
I am not sure of love any more
after the trick it played
slippery, baffling, malicious.
Write it, tell me on paper
that we love each other.

Etheridge Knight

The Idea of Ancestry

1

Taped to the wall of my cell are 47 pictures: 47 black
faces: my father, mother, grandmothers (1 dead), grandfathers (both dead), brothers, sisters, uncles, aunts,
cousins (1st & 2nd), nieces, and nephews. They stare
across the space at me sprawling on my bunk. I know
their dark eyes, they know mine. I know their style,
they know mine. I am all of them, they are all of me;
they are farmers, I am a thief, I am me, they are thee.

I have at one time or another been in love with my mother,
1 grandmother, 2 sisters, 2 aunts (1 went to the asylum),
and 5 cousins. I am now in love with a 7 yr old niece
(she sends me letters written in large block print, and
her picture is the only one that smiles at me).

I have the same name as 1 grandfather, 3 cousins, 3 nephews,
and 1 uncle. The uncle disappeared when he was 15, just took
off and caught a freight (they say). He's discussed each year
when the family has a reunion, he causes uneasiness in
the clan, he is an empty space. My father's mother, who is 93
and who keeps the Family Bible with everybody's birth dates
(and death dates) in it, always mentions him. There is no
place in her Bible for "whereabouts unknown."

2

Each fall the graves of my grandfathers call me, the brown
hills and red gullies of mississippi send out their electric
messages, galvanizing my genes. Last yr / like a salmon quitting
the cold ocean-leaping and bucking up his birthstream / I
hitchhiked my way from L.A. with 16 caps in my pocket and a
monkey on my back. And I almost kicked it with the kinfolks.

I walked barefooted in my grandmother's backyard / I smelled the
    old
land and the woods / I sipped cornwhiskey from fruit jars with the
    men /
I flirted with the women / I had a ball till the caps ran out
and my habit came down. That night I looked at my grandmother
and split / my guts were screaming for junk / but I was almost
contented / I had almost caught up with me.
(The next day in Memphis I cracked a croaker's crib for a fix).

This yr there is a gray stone wall damming my stream, and when
the falling leaves stir my genes, I pace my cell or flop on my bunk
and stare at 47 black faces across the space. I am all of them,
they are all of me, I am me, they are thee, and I have no children
to float in the space between.

For Black Poets Who Think of Suicide

Black Poets should live—not leap
From steel bridges (like the white boys do).
Black Poets should live—not lay
Their necks on railroad tracks (like the white boys do).
Black Poets should seek—but not search too much
In sweet dark caves, nor hunt for snipe
Down psychic trails (like the white boys do).

For Black Poets belong to Black People. Are
The Flutes of Black Lovers. Are
The Organs of Black Sorrows. Are
The Trumpets of Black Warriors.
Let All Black Poets die as Trumpets,
    And be buried in the dust of marching feet.

To Make a Poem in Prison

It is hard
To make a poem in prison.
The air lends itself not
to the singer.
The seasons creep by unseen
And spark no fresh fires.

Soft words are rare, and drunk drunk
Against the clang of keys;
Wide eyes stare fat zeroes
And plead only for pity.

But pity is not for the poet;
Yet poems must be primed.
Here is not even sadness for singing,
Not even a beautiful rage rage,
No birds are winging. The air
Is empty of laughter. And love?
Why, love has flown,
Love has gone to glitten.

Etheridge Knight

Belly Song

(for the Daytop Family)

"You have made something
Out of the sea that blew
And rolled you on its salt bitter lips.
It nearly swallowed you.
But I hear
You are tough and harder to swallow than most . . ."
— S. Mansfield

1

And I   and I / must admit
that the sea in you
    has sung / to the sea / in me
and I   and I / must admit
that the sea in me
    has fallen / in love
    with the sea in you
because you have made something
out of the sea
    that nearly swallowed you

And this poem
This poem
This poem / I give / to you.
This poem is a song / I sing / I sing / to you
from the bottom
    of the sea
        in my belly

This poem
This poem
This poem / is a song / about FEELINGS
about the Bone of feeling
about the Stone of feeling
    And the Feather of feeling

2

This poem
This poem
This poem / is /
a death / chant
and a grave / stone
and a prayer for the dead:
    for young Jackie Robinson.
a moving Blk / warrior who walked
among us
    with a wide / stride — and heavy heels
moving   moving   moving
thru the blood and mud and shit of Vietnam
moving   moving   moving
thru the blood and mud and dope of America
    for Jackie / who was /

a song
and a stone
and a Feather of feeling
    now dead
and / gone / in this month of love

This poem
This poem / is / a silver feather
and the sun-gold / glinting / green hills breathing
river flowing — for Sheryl and David — and
their first / kiss by the river — for Mark and Sue
and a Sunday walk on her grand / father's farm
for Sammy and Marion — love rhythms
for Michael and Jean — love rhythms
love / rhythms — love rhythms — and LIFE.

3

This poem
This poem
This poem
This poem / is / for ME — for me
and the days / that lay / in the back / of my mind
when the sea / rose up /
    to swallow me
and the streets I walked
    were lonely streets
    were stone / cold streets

This poem
This poem / is /
for me / and the nights
    when I
wrapped my feelings
    in a sheet of ice
and stared
    at the stars
        thru iron bars
           and cried
in the middle of my eyes . . .

This poem
This poem
This poem / is / for me
    and my woman
    and the yesterdays
when she opened
    to me like a flower
but I fell on her
    like a stone
I fell on her like a stone . . .

4

    And now — in my 40th year
        I have come here
    to this House of Feelings
    to this Singing Sea
    and I   and I / must admit
    that the sea in me
        has fallen / in love
    with the sea in you
    because the sea
    that now sings / in you
        is the same sea
    that nearly swallowed you —
        and me too.

A Watts Mother Mourns While Boiling Beans

The blooming flower of my life is roaming
in the night, and I think surely
that never since he was born
have I been free from fright.
My boy is bold, and his blood
grows quickly hot / even now
he could be crawling in the street
bleeding out his life, likely as not.
Come home, my bold and restless son. — Stop
my heart's yearning! But I must quit
this thinking — my husband is coming
and the beans are burning.

Etheridge Knight

Sibyl James

Translitics from
The Love Sonnets of Louise Labé

(1)

Search history and the old tales,
those tunes in a blind Greek's throat.
No one before me hurt like this,
not Ulysses, not that witch Circe,
twisting restless on her mat.

Love's a proud god, a slim matador
playing to the stands.
He sets his black heel at my neck.
He lifts his sword hand, empty,
like a deep bow.

Love, your look is a blade of blue flame,
a luxury of heat I dream and die in,
a woman in a drugged fever.
No way out but through your heart.

This is bitter luck. This is that scorpion poison
that seeks the sting again like cure.

Over and over I spit the hot arena sand.
I lift my head and have to rinse my lips again
with yours. Over and over, I lose or lose.

(2)

The game, the moves:

1. two eyes, brown (or maybe any color, just
      lovely)

2. and then you won't look at me

3. hot breath, a wall of it, moving
   like forest fire

4. nights at the kitchen table,
   no candles lit,
   no key turning in the lock

5. so what if the sun comes back,
   that sad calendar of x's on the wall.
   love like a mule, stiff-willed,
   pulling its own way,
   taking the kick in the ribs

6. a thousand trout, breathless,
   thrashing in the tight net

7. take the worst, turn it against me

8. yr. laugh
   yr. head, hair, arms, hand,
   one by one, yr. fingers

9. what sings so rich?
   across the dark street, one violin
   or you on the porch
   bending the blues notes,
   the way you say my name.

Taking the tricks:

You stack the deck to light one woman.
I'm flaming with yr. suit, tiny hearts
you branded on my heart. They blaze,
sparks spill against yr. skin, and die.

(8)

Je vis, je meurs.
Life is the soft palm
cradling my head, the blade
between ribs.
I'm galactic cold where my star burns.
Face down in the lake, my throat
still flaming.

Weeks of street cafes yawn by,
malaise in my tea, fingers
too heavy to crook. And some face
falls sudden over the cup's rim,
some fine cheekbone, a sugar cube
to suck this broth against.

Even the desert blooms sometimes,
big blowzy scents, like fakirs
balanced on a bed of spikes.
That's my spring, mister, that train
leaving either way, and still here.
So don't ask me how I am,
just hand that ragged girl in the gutter
roses, and watch her salt smile,
laughing like all that red must hurt.

Love loves changes, leads me
on a leash. Some days so choked
I get beyond this ache, like breathing.
Some days lying thigh to thigh on white sheets,
the window up, and street noise
slipping in like breeze. I think
the earth's stopped turning, curved perfect
into this late sun. And then that hand
pulling my face close, that old heartbreak
unfolding like a creased schedule of trains.

(19b)

*This is dedicated
to the one I love.*

Downtown, Motown,
Diana's supreme.
All the hot stags shafted
in that cool bar.
She croons at her table
and the background girls
hum in.

Louise
comes in.
A regular.
Head in some cloud
like she had white powder
lately up her nose.

Diana says, "hey, poet.
Hey, I've missed you at my shows.
Girl, sit down
before you fall down.

That scene yr. on
looks dead-end,
and, in case you haven't noticed,
some dude has copped yr. song."

Who should know it
like Louise?
She drops that needle every night
on "Baby Love."

"I emptied the barrel, Diana.
Pitched the gun at his heart."

"He whipped those bullets back
like I was target practice.
Shot me, in the name of love."

(21)

What air in a man sets yr. blood on edge?
Is he '57 chevie punk
or dapper as the Pierce Arrow ad.
Whose thumb jerks you over on the highway?
What eyes, so deep you fall like Alice?
What size, what color, what nose hawk-hungry as
    Dylan's
or uptown straight.
Whose knife so far in yr. heart
no Arthur can wrench it.
What voice tonguing yr. eyes to tears—
the bent E-string blue of it
or raw and ragged as a Southside sax.
What Marlboro tapped from a t-shirt, what
continental cut behind a Gaulois?

What strut, what lift of his hand for a cab,
what slouch, what hip, what shoulder slant, which
side does he sleep on, what rhythm?
How does he stand in doorways?
What face coming up in yr. mirror?
Whose flame in yr. candled eyes?

Poker-faced, I'd play w/o the answers.
But love has forced my hand to where
I need no extras, no
royalty under the table, no fifth ace.
Under yr. touch, my suits all burn to hearts,
under the joker's wild of yr. eyes.

(24)

Don't wag yr. fingers at me, ladies,
if I like a man's hand in the curls
of my permanent wave, if I slip into midnight cafes
and glow like bar light on a crystal of Pernod.

Love brings its own wag.

If a motorcycle gearing to fourth
is nothing to my breathlessness,
winds in Kansas have been nothing to my sighs.
I have run into love so hard
it looks like I painted my toenails blue.
And you w/yr. righteous St. Vitus fingers — nights enough
I've spent starin' down the phone, I don't
need you over the back fence
callin' me up to say
it's a wrong number.

Love, ladies, could slide his hand under yr. elbow
at any crosswalk.
And it might not be no Charles Boyer,
no Mick Jagger for you to protest
you were just danced away.
Could be the blue jay of the postman on his new route.
Could be the guy changin' yr. flat,
the angle of his rolled-back sleeve against yr. fender.
For you, ladies, love might traffic in softer goods
than what hooked me, and still
scratch his visions in yr. waterfall eyes.
Could be you'll howl down canyons
while I stick to the moss and fog of these ravines.

So don't waste yr. fingers, waggin' at me, ladies.
Lay 'em upside yr. eyes like blinders,
like mud-guards against the SLAP of love.

Wendy Wood

I Never Knew It Was You

never knew it was you.
quiet. so slow. and o
smooth, chagall blues
already crowded heart
you'd lived there a
noticed it was snowing
no shoes. wrote songs
even when you moved a
know it was you never
knew whose music ran
my skin you grew like
wall, tiny flowers
rings were worn your
light rain   there was a
garden in my thighs
still didn't know
you came in so
you'd lived there a
night alone with only
bad party, loud and
slamming, thoughts
I saw you, near a window
piano, as if   you'd lived there a
long time and all this time I never knew it was
you never knew it was you

you came in so
so river water
you came in an
made room as if
long time. no one
outside you wore
near a window not
piano in did I
knew you came in
through my bones over
ivy on a stone
bloomed where
lips like
one morning I
it was you
quiet as if
long time. then that
my heart a
people leaving, doors
crowding the bed
playing a

She Leaves

she can just pick up & leave
anytime she wants she can just
pick up & leave & leave pieces
of something everywhere/ in ohio
she left a man in ohio in boston
she left another & another in
chicago & it's not always men sometimes it's her
self in manhattan she leaves her
self on corners in the   strangest places
she left a shoe & a poem in nevada one
time she left a note on a bed a lot of
times she don't look back she knows that's
nowhere & likes where she's at when she's
there & loves to look at what
lies ahead if it's a man or
someplace else she
wrote this poem in the middle of a street in
soho while   rearranging her wings while
planning on picking up &
leaving it's always like

fall for her

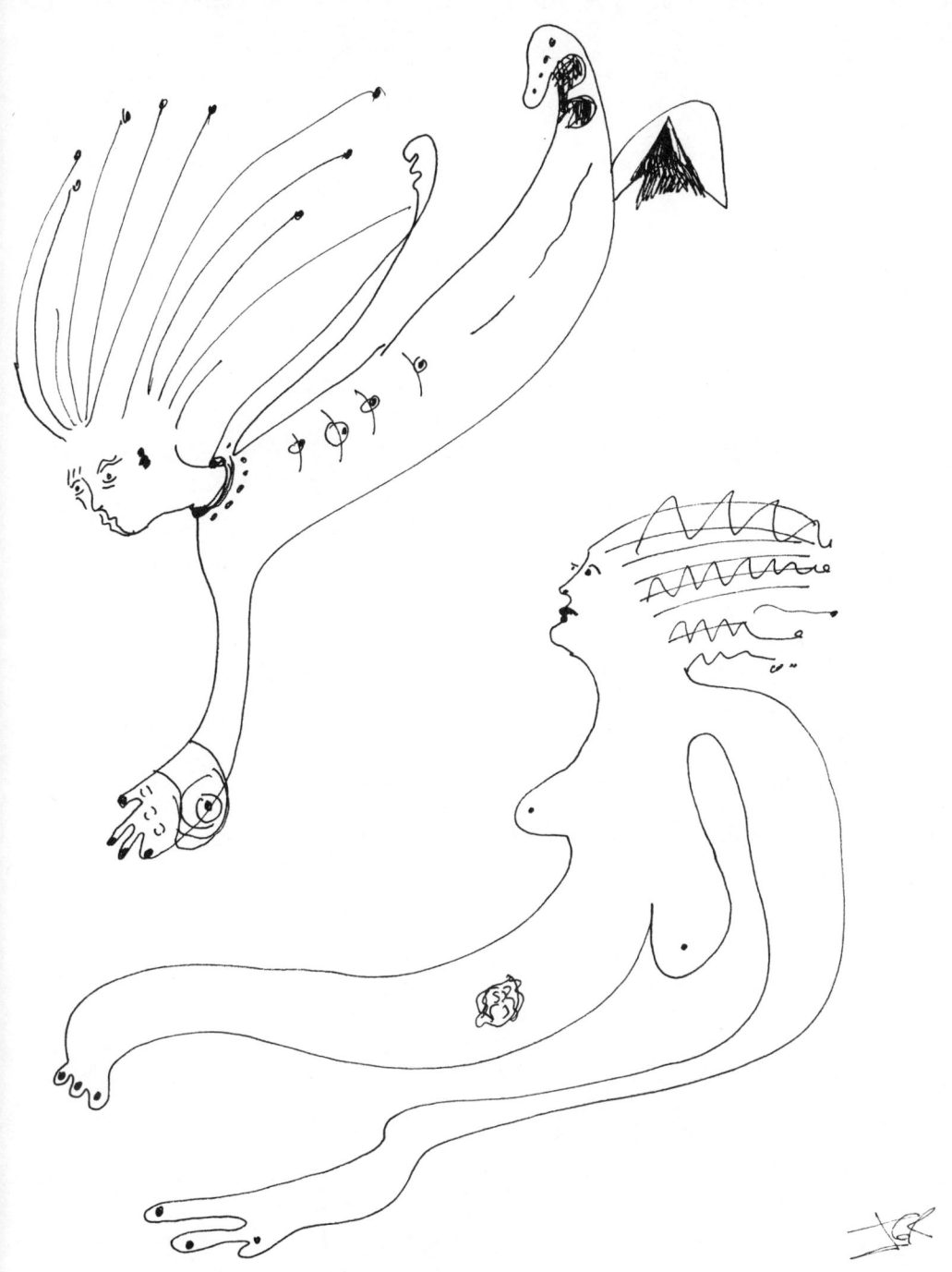

MYTH

Carrie Allen

Maximum Occupied Armor

This was no knight on white stallion.
I heard no medley nor saw the moon
But here was this fat boy
In the corner
Laughing, despite himself,
At some sort of inner symphony
Like a symphony within a seashell
In fine, pink-walled peristyles
On a doolittle day.
And this, I suppose, is
Medley and moon enough
For me.
—No dream
No need—
When this young boy conducts
Such a pleasant feast of tunes
To which, if I listen hard,
I can still hear
This far from the sea.

E. R. Gregory

Story of Q

(1)

Pierre had beaten her with the slim black riding crop
for eight hours (would that he would never stop!)
"How he must love me," she sobbed as she bled
all over the iron-spiked bed.

(2)

Of course it's only my opinion, but
I've sometimes thought that slim black riding crops
were old-hat as porno props
and that I've fathomed her secret: she's a nut.

They Laughed at Sappho

They laughed at Sappho and thought her quite the fool
For taking sweet young things into her so-called school,
But when they learned what she was teaching there,
The laughter turned to snide remarks about her purple hair.

The dolts! How little could they understand
The legacy she'd brought their sun-burned land:
If in a sense she'd made the girls unfit
For mother-, wife-, and livelihood,
She'd nonetheless bestowed a kind of grace
Upon the island wood
And made a gift of song to all the Grecian race.

Culture

is like a fragile comtesse
of the oldest, bluest blood.
Each night by a secret passageway
she admits to her boudoir
Pierre the groomsman.

Pierre is large, well-built, hairy.
His fingernails are torn and dirty.
He smells of the stable.
Before he lays her
he beats her black and blue.

By day Mme la Comtesse is
cool, distant, untouchable.
As she rides past on the chestnut mare
Pierre touches his cap
but she ignores him.
N'importe. He knows that in the evening
she will lie beneath him
panting, avid, screaming . . . .

Yep folks that's culture.

Martin Willitts, Jr.

Ma And Pa Kettle Meet Godzilla

The earth shakes on the wide screen
under terrible lizard feet
and pools of lakes are formed
where ice melts in misty light

but Pa Kettle is too busy rocking
figuring his next checker move,
his jaw working a wad of tobacco,
a fly bothering his nose, he never blinks

the Japanese run for air raid shelters
like ants returning to their mounds,
they buzz like broken transistor waves
and English words appear under their feet

but Ma counts her children using fingers
and toes, losing count, forgetting names,
her fingers smell of blueberry pies
baked fresh for county fair blue ribbons

flames spit out of Godzilla's mouth
as missiles bounce off his thick skin,
he swats planes like bothersome flies
and crushes papermache houses with his feet

Pa adjusts the derby on his head
and Ma unties her apron strings,
Godzilla flattens their beat up truck
not covered by any insurance

but the kids, outnumbering the Japanese,
armed with sling shots, skip ropes, biting,
snot dripping from their running noses,
they tie Godzilla in knots Houdini can't untie

the kids ride Godzilla like a broken horse
with whimpering tail between his legs,
as Ma tries to count all the kids
and Pa still plans his next checker move

Jesse James Becomes Bogart

You must remember this,
a kiss is but a kiss,
but a broad is dangerous
full of fast curves
and no exits. They leave you
after they crush a cigarette
beneath blood red finger tip,
and return when you've forgotten
those nights in hot Paris
sticking to each other.
They bring dead bodies
like luggage.
The piano plays when she enters
and there is no piano,
just her in a white dress.
The color does not suit her.
She should be wearing black,
black as the night in her heart,
black as the marks she left
on my back, black as her kisses,
black as the fingerprints
smudged on her false passport.
Now she wants you, sweetheart.

Martin Willitts, Jr.

She wants you to be the fall guy,
to take the bullet meant for her
as kind of a farewell present.
Then she will leave fresh
as perfume and just as deadly.
Well, here's looking at you kid.
It's the same old story.
Boy meets girl, girl gets boy killed
and disappears into the fog
riding an airplane, as time goes by.
But not this time fella.
I'm not taking the fall.
We will say its the fat man
or his friend with the saucer eyes.
No, she's the one going to take a fall.
She did it with delicate fingers
wearing kid white gloves.
She is going over and I'm sending her.
This time she will get the big sleep.

Eugene Marino

Elegy for Colonial Press

Rest in peace Carini and Bill Hamm,
Ziggy and Killer Kilcoyne.
Rest in peace the joker
who crayoned "Transfer to Poland"
and "Transfer to the Raebu Room"
on the prototype transfer form.

Colonial Press, Clinton, Massachusetts,
a raucous symphony of a thousand
clanging away between sheet-metal walls.
Textbooks and trash novels hot off
thundering presses. Workers sweating
through faded green and blue and white T-shirts,
signatures marching like white army ants,
25,000 an hour off the Cotrell, the same
off Number 8 rubber rotary,
Number 6 slow as shit and molasses
and older than Tommy Walsh, its pressman,
but still spitting out books.

Come on, Colonial Press, don't you crack
a smile when you remember Carini
overwhelmed by the flow of books
from Number 8, falling behind,
scattering signatures in a semi-circle
around his tray and yelling
"I'm so fucking glad" when
the roll tender missed a paster
on the fly and the broken web
flapped through the press?

And can't you just see Bill Hamm
pounding his fist in hopeless lust
on a thousand-pound roll
of Kennebec's best when
that secretary with dress
hugging ass walks by?
Or Ziggy picking his nose and chuckling
while reading the latest smut
from Ballentine, mouthing
"this is the good part"
with the press roaring
and straining three feet away?
Or Killer Kilcoyne armwrestling
all comers, his thin face a watery red,
his bicep a softball-sized hillock?

Dream, Colonial Press,
it's all you have left,
for the new skipper
didn't like the cut of your jib
and scuttled you at sea,
leaving your complement of a thousand
to scurry like rats.
Widows stand on the bayshore
keening, but we know your epitaph
is shorter and sweeter
than a woman's wail.
Yet how vulgarly it rolls off the tongue:
tax writeoff.

Why Italians didn't invent the wristwatch

In the small frame house
plum-tomato steam
calls on every corner,
    gently tugs
each separate heart
and stomach
to table.

It is twelve noon,
    Sunday.

a father viewed from 800 miles

I.

I picture him in his T-shirt,
jeans of dung and dust, mind
like a pitchfork, his awl
of a nose in a newspaper,
slurping coffee at the kitchen table

Funny, his face bears no scar
of a youth that careened
from Clinton to Tokyo Bay,
from brutal ballet on a canvas
square to Kamikaze shuffle.
Always lucky

except when unlucky.
Like the time he had a black bear
in his sights,
and the safety on.
Or when he wrestled a washing
machine down the cellar stairs.
His wrist pulsed dark blood

Blood that recalled
latifundium and Roman legion
probably the Peloponnesus too
Blood that reeked of garlic surprised
in hot olive oil, of peeled plum
tomatoes, basil and rigatoni,
of peperonata and peperoni

II.

I picture him on his knees
hands moist and black to the wrist
soil oozing between fingers
filling his nails, slipping into
shoes and socks and pants, a mound
for squash taking shape
in rock-besotted soil
that would make a Puritan faint-hearted

And always gifts for birds
birds and more birds
shitting on front lawn and back
Cardinals come to feed, goldfinch
and wren, jay and dove and sparrow
always songs of disparate birds
and the dissonance of his craggy
voice rumbling in the back of his
throat with some private tune

III.

I picture him in a cocoon
of wires, transistors, bright
tubes, a hospital ward
of naked televisions, alone
in his shop in the evening
his hazel eyes glistening
with the intricacies of his work.

Electricity at once charges him
and shorts his strength
so that at nine
he climbs the stairs
and lays himself into his easychair,
eyes shut, thin lips at ease,
breath slow and deep, slow and deep

Marisella Viega

Hereditary Curse

I am part of your children's bedtime
story as they sit around the campfire
in uniform, shooting glances into the pine
waiting for the wind to whittle
a face from bark, for the needles
to soften into hair.

I am your darling werewolf,
the one you meet at a party,
the one who follows you home,
crawls with permission, into your bed.
Why bother fastening windows?
Cementing tiles to the floor?
Werewolf brewing some coffee,
earning the key to your door.

I am already
that hidden box of bon bons
your maybe parachute
your widening eyes at the shake
of these dice
signal the werewolf in you.

Snarl at the sun in the morning.
Neptune will be our moon.
The hairs on our limbs will thicken,
a heavy yarn the villagers
will stare at, and quickly gather
their children into some sturdy room.

State Fair

A bald man selling leather
from inside a hut hires me.
He puts no forms in my hands,
does not look at my knees or palms
for calluses, tells me I
must not touch, and gives me a pole
to pluck purses from hooks in the ceiling.

I stand all day and half the night
guarding the stiff shapes and holsters.

He pays me. I walk to the booths
where woolen blankets cover the walls,
finger the one I've chosen and hand
a dollar to the woman who knows
I will own it before winter.

I pass the rides where people scream
and curse and pray,
pass the tent with the lucky cow:
two heads, a millionaire already!

And every night I see Bob and George,
their heads stationary before a window
as people climb the steps of a trailer
to stare then maybe rage at God
or pity that misfortune:
two males joined at birth, forever one.

I marvel at the strength of their shared organs.

Marisella Viega

Flamingos

Days ago I saw you in a photograph.
You, eating out of my aunt's hand,
she, laughing, as you tickled her palm
while she sat outdoors at a table.

I see you now,
on this paper, behind this glass,
and wonder which stem in
Emmanuel's heart you have sprung from.

You have come to the north
this winter, to a land as foreign
to you as the color in
the body of these skies,
a land where it is difficult
to take the farmer's eyes away
from the white on his fields.

Flamingos,
you urge me to pull my kite
from the closet and fly it,
a palm against the grey,
a womb against the clouds,

already my ankles are in water!

Marisella Viega

Marilyn L. Pinheiro

Siren Song

I live alone.
No one speaks to me
but winter wind.
I hear his whisper,
husky, hoarse and teasing
just outside my door.
His voices are an orchestra,
drum and violin,
bass and oboe,
flute and cello
haunting me.
Seductively he moans,
crooning siren songs.
He blows me messages
inscribed on dry oak leaves,
curled papyrus
resurrected from a tomb,
crumbling when I
try to read them.
Suddenly the wind is silent,
pausing, listening.

I unbolt the door
and walk into
his wild embrace.

Margaret A. Weber

Silent Things

I prowl through silence in my house at night,
Bare feet caressed by rugs and polished floor.
The piano now seems more than wood and wire,
On tensioned loom, weft snuggles into warp.
I sit upon a chair's lap, stroke its arms,
Then glide to bed, and like a grownup ghost,
Recall the child who waved a long goodnight
To toys and table, rocking horse and boat,

Far further back, the emerging human's awe
Of beasts bright painted on a dark cave wall.

Ray Gene Patrick

dream #6

I undrape the mummy bound rags
tangled
each marked
with vibration & self interest
dust & dryed wine.
one eye surveys the room
a square of rust-grey
a vapor trail called the past
your portrait hangs on one wall
cream & blue
its face
looks sideways
the direction you have taken
& points
like an ax
cutting the empty air.

key west motor momma

motor momma
on your motorcycle daddy's
black leather back
hang on baby
your sweet ass
rides the highway
like a wet thigh painting
you smile a secret
a tattoo on your belly
a pointed arrow
a nose stuffed full
of magic
white moon dust
your father cries
from his suburban home chains
but he'll never have your body
motor momma freedom
desire driven
past cities
towns
curbs
where you watch the other people
your heart is a chrome chain
your eyes are
hot liquid armpits
screaming
like a lost phoenix in flight

Peter van Schaick

from *The Landscape Between Us is the Dream of Oceans*

Mount Palomar Observatory

You don't have to be on this mountain
To roll the doors down from the roof of the dome
And focus on the oceans of mind

Like fishermen on a starry night by the sea,
As wave after wave after wave
Of phosphemic geysers spew into galaxies,

Evanescent star clusters and clouds
Flower from seeds of light
Divining for water through geological substrata

Glabrous bamboo shoots of muscle, vein, and bone
To the blastoids under the footprints
That entrench us like roots to the rough escarpment

Of implacable cliffs dominating
And retreating from the flux and reflux
Of pounding surf: ladies fingers, feathers,

White caps, white horses, and skippers' daughters.
Single bursts of light reflect and defract
And copulate into multi-cellular ideas and feelings

And dreams of wave upon wave lapping up
Against the bones under the dome of the skull
Grinding and shaping and sculpting

The smooth basins of interior passageways,
Chiseling and hollowing out niches and crevasses,
Moulding sockets that collect bowls of light

Filled with Peary's white roses
And holes for the singing and buzzing of bees.

Hydrometer

A quelle heure descendez le Bathysphere?
Backstroking through this river of stars
We almost open our eyes and see ourselves

Children swimming in the womb of the mind.
Look at the snapshots: an ochre hand blown through a tube
Outlined on a wall at Altimira or Lescaux;

Dissolve to a Cycladic fertility goddess, you are Ishtar;
Cut to a flying apsara from Tun-Huang fluttering in the sun
Like a dragonfly over the Silk Route; the breath

Of Wu-Tao-tzu in a memory of fog drifting through pine
    forests;
The whole series of Rembrandt self-portraits; color
    membranes
of Kandinsky; and Pollocks overlapping the edge of the
    canvas;

Sun Obelisks and Wind Gyrators; Sappho, Lalla, and
    Neobule;
The desert bones of Georgia O'Keefe; Sophie Drinker:
Such a fertile dinner party of multifloriate imaginings.

Goldfish and carp flying over waterfalls like blimps,
Plum blossoms dropping through rainbows over the sea
Of Marmor, splicing into the film of ourselves

Spinning, reeling, and unreeling like kelp
Drawn from the depths and the sound of the sea at Nootka,
Looping to Rio and to Arista in the Gulf of Tehuantepec,

To Bahia de Ballenas in Baja California Sur.
El Nino blows updrafts through windows
Of pistils and stamens of eyes on stalks

Peering through golden filaments lacing the interior dome
Of the Blue Mosque: we listen synaptically flashing
We hear wailing, we feel neurons dance;

Bellies slide past dreams unfolding
Thighs filled with honey swim to other oceans
Of you and me wave after wave of ourselves

Arm and back, rowing 20 billion light years around the
    middle,
A unified field of sound in the mouth
Through the lips, one breath, waaaaaaaaaaaaahhh;

An isochronal fugue of ebbing and flowing; tidal changes
Surge from the belly of oceans billowing and swelling with
    milk,
Lapping the dunes of the coast.

A toccata of dolphins arc above the sea surface
In counterpoint with young balleens: spewing water
And taking soundings, they undulate downward

Passing through black rainstorms of light that flash to Papua
Along the ocean floor. At sunrise they slide
Through rhomboidal nets and swim

Down the coastal fjords at Yakutat Bay
Into the Gulf of Alaska, southward
To the warmth of the middle earth.

Aztlan

Bronze Virgin, your dark face wrestling with stone
Shadows cast by the setting sun, your eyes were two halves

Of a full moon, your mind a Stradivarius dense
With impacted light. The volcano gushes straight from the
    heart

And you spread the lava like lotion over your glowing skin.
All I could think about was coming and coming and coming

In the cool fountains under the Aztec Sunwheel, and never
Going or turning. She smiled at me in the obsidian mirror

Through the black river of her hair and swam on
Through the spring sky, beyond the Great Triangle,

A swan heading south, brushing the Harp with her wings
Moving into Scorpio, giving birth to twins.

Toledo, Ohio

Our dreams are here in Toledo, Ohio
Slipping and sliding and slopping
Between the oceans of ourselves and the memory of swamps.

There is nothing anywhere that is not here:
Thunder Egg agates that drop from the Rockies
And roll like bowling balls across the flatlands

Peter van Schaick

And through back alleys of Toledo, Ohio
But nobody notices; all the gods and goddesses
From Tibet Mexico Lebanon Italy India Toledo

Are right here, making music become space
In parking lots of breakdancers tuned
To Crazy Artists FM asking questions

About the kind of fish coming out of their faucets.
Everyone I know who has left Toledo is back:
The rivers and lakes flow uphill out of town and

All hitch-hikers in the area are now cocoons of fulgerite,
Lightning-fused sand; the rainbow factory makes housecalls
For vaginal implants; whale meat is used for hotdogs.

Is it true that only dolphins and whales swim
From one ocean to another, but they have to go
Through the Port of Toledo to get there?

And of course we know that they sing to each other
From thousands of miles away, but only recently
Has it been discovered that these songs are

Hypersonic transliterations of Theresa Brewer hits.
At Banner Mattress I have heard that they are hawking
Icelandic feldspar and rutilated quartz

Filled with diodes, phosphorescent snails, and oolite,
Helpful if you want your waterbed to double as an aquarium.
The mountains in Toledo are on the moonstone

Buried under the sun obelisk in Promenade Park;
And the Sung Dynasty vases that are so wonderful
To breathe along with, well, they're wonderful

To breathe along with and they seem to smile at you
As single brushstrokes flash across white surfaces.
There are smiles like that in Toledo, Ohio.

Peter van Schaick

Howard T. Parker

Puttin' on the Fat

As the golden sunrise
Invades morning,
Hunger pains declare
War with my stomach . . .

One dozen fresh country eggs
Two pounds of lean smoked bacon
Twenty-four butter-milk flap-jacks
    "Puttin' on the Fat" . . . .

In between . . my stomach feels lean
Two bags of Lay's potato chips
Five Hershey bars . . . five cracker-jacks
    "Puttin' on the Fat" . . . .

Crunch . . Crunch . . Crunch
    Time out for lunch . . .
Two dozen fresh ocean perch
Six baked Idaho baked potatoes in butter
One Boston creme pie
Six slices of longhorn cheese
Aged not too sharp . . not too flat
    "Puttin' on the Fat" . . . .

Dinner is a winner
Five pound broiled black angus rib steak
Six cans of imported Chinese vegetable soup
One bowl of fresh-tossed salad
One quart of French vanilla ice cream
One six pack of L.A. beer . . one bottle of
    imported Rémy cognac,
Guess I'll have to change my plan tonight
    And stay where I'm at,
Because I'm puttin' on
    Too damn much fat . . .

Dream-Green

Some parks in New York City
      are DREAM GREEN,

When strolling through the park
      If you're not careful your pockets
         are PICKED CLEAN . . .

People aren't always mean
      if they dream-green;

The hills of Kentucky are DREAM-GREEN
      People mining, drinking and their
         clothes always need a washing . . .

Gene wheeled on the scene in a
      DREAM-GREEN-ZODIAC CADILLAC
Along the curb set ten junkers
      every damn tire flat

The dream-green-zodiac machine
      Was out of place like a Catholic nun
         at Studio 54, BREAK DANCING . . .

Jeff Olma

from *The Wet Deck Poems*

there is a story
that once
there was a small band of sailors
who were so lost
so off their prescribed course
that everything was new
that the new was familiar
after a fashion,
that even silence had a sound,
gloved as it was.

it is said
that the story never got out.

§

when they were lost
the world was one gigantic Macy's
with a john somewhere in the back.

they couldn't even find their way
out of the housewares section
and who wants a damn doorbell anyway?
the maps said.

it always starts in science.

somebody reads
about the percentage of water
in man
and so they float
on the patched inner tubes
of their inheritance
making a brave putt   putt   putt . . .

§

According to Jane's Fighting Ships
the Ipso Calypso
looks exactly
like nothing
you've ever seen
before . . .

Fig 2   An Early photo

§

Jeff Olma

the day's first business
was a public flogging of navigation,
witnessed by the crew
and a majority of officers.

". . . it is hereby adjudged inhumane
and masochistic to sail by the stars
due to the fact
that the vessel has an aviation incapacity.

". . . therefore, i — mon capatin —
have elected to measure the voyage
by sea birds
should they be sighted.
i will insist that land is nearby
regardless of position
or prevailing winds.

". . . also, while i think of it,
i crave swiss cheese . . ."

§

here's our official portrait —
taken at the precise moment
we sign on.
there's larry
with his davy crockett coonskin cap,
the tail over his nose
like a furry windshield wiper,
cooky in white cap and silver ladle,
pierre in campaign tammy and riding crop,
and capten
with his bligh mask on, pacing
back and forth —
shouting *Missssster Christ-yan*!
look close.
you're seeing us
at our very best.

§

Text of an open letter to Charles Darwin
and the crew of the HMS BEAGLE drawn up
by the crew of the IPSO CALYPSO in the
event that we should somehow meet . . .

Dearests,
We could save you
much time and bother.
Telephone 738-1596 toll free.
Ask for any one of us.

§

our sextant
is an old gold picture frame.

to know where we are
we simply place it
before our eyes
and let it catch
a small fish of earth
in its nets.

sometimes
we are equidistant from the eyes
of someone's muttonchops
stern great grandfather
stymied in portrait pose.

sometimes
we are at the centre
of an indistinct moment.

sometimes
we see what we see
with only one collective crew's eye.

picture that
can you
picture that
can you?

Jeff Olma

§

everything is the first nice morning
in june
here.

larry oils his mitt
then rides his bike
to the playground —
leagues away.

pierre is the paperboy.
he gives everybody a break
and doesn't collect.

he is a marksman
with his news tosses.

one doorstep
has THE EAGLE HAS LANDED!
another — next to a milkbox —
has MERRY CHRISTMAS ALL!
a dog carries MAZ' HOMER DOES IT!
YANKS CAN'T BELIEVE!

there are no obituaries
in the papers. only hats
and fans and french fries
and well-folded planes.

§

the Ipso is doldrumed.
"so okay," larry the morale officer yells,
"lets have a picnic!"

pierre unfurls
the red and white checkered picnic blanket,
tents the foredeck,
anchors the sheet at opposite corners
with his big black boots.

larry breaks out
the badminton, the bocci ball,
the horselatitude shoes;

and cooky makes the mess —
there is chicken and sweet ghurkins
and black greek olives
and Hamm's on tap
and crystal radios
with the All Star Game
at the top of the first,
and cukes and radishes
cayenne and pepper
and *real* lemonade
with bits of lemon floating in it
like shards of flavor,
and hot apple pie
and neopolitan ice cream
and steamy brazilian coffee
and appetites armed with german potato salad.

and there is a silly sadness:
no ants.

§

a woman comes aboard

the first agreement
was that her name
was not important.

she had thin wrists
and had hands
that always reached
short.

at the evening meal
she was put to
putting cream on
everything. what?
a mess? she said?

she was magic
because in a way
she stayed
and was with us
more
after she left.

§

later,
above us, the stars move
like a math equation
in a slow child's mind:

they are a merry-go-round
of retarded light.

we
the nodding horse,
you
the copper rings.

Jeff Olma

§

special duty. our routine changes.
morale is high: Amy, daughter of the admiral,
is due on the 7th like a holiday.

we have been chosen
to be her home away from daddy —
her playroom and doll house.

our immediate task
is to batte, secure, and rennovate —
there is not very much time
and Amy is a very particular child.

first, there is the paint job.
she *just adores* powder blue and puce,
so the Ipso dons the hues,
strutting the joke like a painted woman.

the engine room
is her toybox, astrew with pooh and tygger,
and dominoes spelling a. . .m. . .y. . .
a stationary red tricycle
and a home-viewer's edition of The Dating Game.

the Ips's profile is wicker stroller.
its course looks for a nice city park
rimmed with daffodils.

foredeck grows rosegardens
and trellises next to swings.

capn donates his very own copy
of Alice in Wonderland,
pierre practices his juggling,
concentrating especially on his linguini trick,
and larry hides the clearies of his marbles.

§

Jeff Olma

Larry's the Bach of making codes.

he makes a telegraph machine
out of soup pots, wiring,
and three decks of water pipe.

he does semophore
and smoke signals
in copper and aluminum.

our ears ring with his inspiration.

the sound creates mirages
in our hearing.
he dances as he performs
like a slo-mo Jerry Lee Lewis.

he finishes
with a rousing rendition
of The Bells of St Marys.

half way through
the pipes freeze
and the song gets laryngitis.

but there is no reMorse in that.

§

Jeff Olma

in the radio room
a message snags us:

RE IPSO CALYPSO.
Row row row your
boat, gently
down the stream;
merrilly, merrilly
merrilly, merrilly
your life is but
a dream. COPY.

§

for the next few months
the Ipso was taxi for hire—
carrying Hussars to the Outback,
Huks to Finland, Yaquis
to the Azores, and accountants
to Atlantis . . .

§

Lynne Walker

from *Big Red*

Dirty Work

I am working nights at a bar
where I clean and clear tables,
slop glasses through three sinks,
watch the same drunk
fall off the same stool
three nights in a row,
and sweep up peanut shells
at 2:00 in the morning.

My husband is on strike
from beer truck driving.
He throws beer cans on the floor
and his dirty socks.
It is against his principles
and his union to work.
So I work
nights in a bar.

At 2:30 in the morning my home is
a vacuum sweeper standing
unused from the afternoon
when the kids got muddy,
dirty dishes in stale sink water,
laundered clothes balled up on the couch,
and a pouchy drunk
who wants to know why I am late.

My husband is on strike
and I don't have time.
Make-up takes time.
Make-up must be exact
when you work nights in a bar;
hot russet eyeliner,
mean green eyeshadow,
beyond red lipstick,
or the face fades away
in bar light.

I clean up after men at the bar.
They don't throw beer cans,
but they pitch lines.
One is a fairly rich persuader
who drinks blackberry brandy
and watches me like a nervous Doberman.

A Reynolds Road motel
is where I am special.
Pandered to and plied with scotch.
I'm so impressive
he cannot get an erection.

Somehow, his failure is appealing,
a hook for a dirty work woman.
That he is not pretty,
has a leather face, ape hands,
finger wavy hair,
is not important.
He does not look like a savior,
but in the tinny tune
filtering through thin walls,
I hear Hosanna.

Big Red Does Michigan Wedding

Fill it!

        Gin and orange juice at 4:30 p.m.
        orange blossoms
        conservative, punch drinking, church going
        hard working farmers, and farmer's wives
        watch Red slop up gin
        and strut her purple and black
        highly slit self to the bar

fill it

        the band don't start till 9:30
        then the partying begins, she is assured
        but Red is here and the party starts
        when she does

fill it

        gradually old farmers are replaced by young
        open necked plaid shirts and pastel housedresses
        become bib overalls and fitted designer jeans
        Red grabs gin with bright long nails
        sashaying to orange blossoms

fill it

        the rock band brought to startle Michigan
        playing hard and bad, undanceable rhythms
        don't stop Big Red's show
        her choreographed black bottom

fill it

        a drunk bold, forward farmer
        cops a feel of her crotch
        wild eyed farmers are blurred
        but Red can't quit provoking

Lynne Walker

fill it

    orange blossoms
    razzle dazzle

    Red quietly leave takes
    black and purple wrinkle the floor
    at 4:00 a.m.
    make-up dirties a washcloth
    home to empty

        fill it

Big Red Cherry

First time it was lost
in a purple mohair pullover,
peter pan lilac blouse,
straight purple skirt to match, of course,
long leg panty girdle, padded bra
and saddle oxfords

    I kept wondering
    what Cousin Judy would think
    an evil girl
    was in love
    did Judy ever give it up for love?
    did she lose
    her unmarried purity for it?

I resisted so long
he'd get a knot in his stomach
his balls were all tight and blue
and probable heart attack insues prolonged petting
he said

Lynne Walker

I had to save him
in the back of an old dark green '53 Chevy
with my one true love
under the walnut tree
in a field, in the car
at midnight and serious
serious about love and sacrifice

I felt I'd been impaled for love
bled and forever tainted for it

Am I a woman yet?

Next time it was lost,
It can happen!
in a slinky, sleasy slit outfit
braless with black crotchless panties
in a phone booth
with Clark Kent who
was not a sacrifice
but a delight

The Bald People, Tony Orlando and Henry Miller

The family down the street
have absolutely no hair.
It's genetic.
They can't help being bald,
but we are freaked out by them,
their goofy wigs, lack of eyebrows.
We get almost hysterical when we try
imagining their genitals.
We call them "the Wigheads" behind their backs
and joke about what planet they sprang from.
We don't want to get close to them.
It is uncomfortable to be kind.

Tony Orlando doesn't have to be sickening.
It is not genetic.
He has chosen phoniness as a vocation,
cultivated the sloppy mediocrity he espouses.
We do not get hysterical about him,
rather we feel like throwing up over him.
We never have to get close to Tony Orlando,
thank God,
and are uncomfortable only as long
as it takes to switch the T.V. station.

Henry Miller would not be uncomfortable
with either of the above.
He was always able to call a freak a freak,
and a cunt a cunt.

Lynne Walker

Big Red Answers Questions Haiku

If you want inside
my thick invisible wall
pack very large lunch

Yes, I do slow dance,
but I don't sip wine slowly
I am a gulper

Fast talk has reasons
It's difficult to refute
inane chattering

You just want inside
my thick magnificent thighs?
possibility

I'm hiding in here
Hey coward, you wanta play
little hide and seek?

I will follow you
if you can get out in front
I run mighty fast

Flashiness is better
than fittering days away
inconsequential.

Sitting still is hard
it makes me contemplate my
gurgling unease

Reinforce your seams
to go dancing with Big Red.
Tie your pants down good.

If I'm all pretense,
why am I so intriguing
to you honest men?

Jack-in-the-box love.
I pop up and you push down.
Who is turning crank?

I was young one time
and for a few scant moments
felt exactly right.

Lynne Walker

Coming Home From Wampler's Lake

Going to Wampler's Lake
after twenty years,
you know you can't go home again.
Maybe your home isn't a home.
Maybe your home is two obnoxious teenagers
with hair in new places, zits, loud voices,
and poor taste in music and friends.

Maybe your home is a lover
who also went to Wampler's Lake.
Who wanders with you through years of picnics,
sand in the ass of bathing suits,
pouring salt on leeches,
fantasies about what the two people way out there
are really doing in the lake,
watching half naked people
and wondering about stories to go with them.

Maybe your home is those teenagers
and that lover,
and his little boy who walks bare naked,
hands behind his back, casually
meeting people, the way you wish you could meet people.
Who will finally let you hold him in the water today,
and who just now,
as you are riding through cornfields,
and the sun has set,
and billions of crickets are clicking,
as you drive from Wampler's Lake,
tired and irritated,
he says to you:
Look at the moon! You see that? You see that moon?

And maybe you think your home is in a car right now,
coming from Wampler's Lake.
But, you knew that.

Lynne Walker

Frumpy and Dumpy Spend Memorial Day in Bed

drinking beer
eating black and green olives
Tony Packo pickles

Frumpy and Dumpy think
they are beautiful
they don't know
they are Frumpy and Dumpy

they believe that she is Rhonda Fleming
or Rita Hayworth
they believe that he is
a brilliant Cary Grant

the frumpy housewife
her dumpy janitor boyfriend
are in an enchanted cottage
reciting "How Do I Love Thee"

they are transformed
perhaps they are
Robert and Elizabeth Browning

Joel Lipman

from *Translitics*

The Real Ideal

Eh, you want to buy a sweating negro?
Come around back past the Chinese tea roses
& I'll show you some hot arms & legs,
one with a belly wet as the ocean.

Eh, you want a cupboard vast as God's brow,
fragrances from the spice shoppe,
air foul as a drunkard's morning fart?
I can put on a platter fit for Bar Mitzvah!

You like to dance allegro or presto,
stroll to the Del-Vikings? Pedro,
I got a palomino out back & a Chevy 409
in the carport. Varooom, my hands are clean as talcum.

If I sound like a skinflint merchant,
crusty as an armadillo without the kiss of a poet,
you're right. But look, jack,
you want tomato-flavored aspirin, I got 'em,

you want vapors from the Pope's mass, I got that.
Some folks pride themselves on piety
& others hoe purple gardens of eggplant.
Me, I'd hustle mama's bridgework for a buck,

then sell her back the breeze she sucks.
Eh, you want Coca Cola from Albania
or lettuce dusted with Modesto radium?
In this land anything goes — you get what you get.

Alone at Jojo's

Nothing is worse
than sitting under a hanging philodendron
with a pizza, alone—
not in Rio,
not in Milano,
but in Findlay, Ohio.

The wine is warm and wretched,
more squeezed from a boil
than poured from a bottle,
and surrounded by vile, sexed-up teenagers
eating mint patties and throwing french fries,
if I was a saboteur, you know
what I'd do. Listen,

Jojo's never hoped to be a spicy cathedral.
These grapes and chianti bottles
arrived in dust, and once
the filthy first owner unloaded
on Manny laPasta and his abominable wife
the joint fell fast
as a cat down the well.
Why am I here tonight,

like last night, and the one before,
awful hours of
eating this stuff,
evening upon evening
licking grease from my thumb,
dumb, drunk on Paisano—
dedicated to:
Jojo's Pizzeria,
Findlay, Ohio

MY LOVE is

                    a saint,
                              a lustre of
                                earth
            comely as   the milk   of   palestine

                              she is   a   palimpsest,
                    a fatal guest,   the branches of
                                              her body

                    a bibliography of   jets &   crevasses

        my love is a grande route,
          the autobahn without ghosts,

                                rumour   of
                        a thousand   lovers   curves her lips

        what a long melancholy gash   of   love
                    when she drops   herself upon the   couch

                              the child   abandoned
                                    to my care

            a party of haute coiture,   carried in   by the   valet
                who says "don't touch, don't touch   the silver bells

                              of those   russet nipples!"

she is the sentry after fornication
        the mountain of gems
            the immobile air —

                                    i am   nothing,   perhaps

            a little farm boy
                        carrying eggs to market

Joel Lipman

Anne Frank

Freud would have called her life a temple,
a divine religion, a flight of columns.
She would be the archangel's mother
had she survived adolescence.

But the camps were around the corner.
Her vision good, the general's better,
and the german shepherd's nosehairs trembled.
God, what music.

So we have a photo, magenta
around the edges, unmistakable Hebrew.
The banks of the Rhine overflow with silver.
Black crepe flutters from the window.

Low Priced Romance

When sober, we reunite, this time you
lean against the hotelroom door while I
succumb on the soft straps of the luggage stand.
We've diluted ourselves to water and carbon.
All night you warmly beat me with snakeskin
till I was the color of antique leather
with a tint of death, a sunset calling
children home in russet afterglow.
The divine rays! I don't know if my groin
aches with the blue strain of boyhood or
god has entered me in this cheap flop.
Dragons in the windowmolding smile down,
the firing squad lounges against the wall
in the courtyard below, the wine is cheap
and bitter as a short peace — but what the hell,
we are emaciated, scurrying like cucarachas
from scrap to scrap. We are in love.

An EXIT sign burns through the wall.
Your pants collapsed in the corner, who
would know you for a brash guerilla, flesh
between the crosshairs of your bandolera?
Why is there a bowl of pig rind on the mantle?
And that third boot under the chair, oh my love,
I will say uncle and be obedient, I won't squeal.
Enough of this sniveling, I feel like thin milk.
My children gathered outside the gate,
7,9,8, and others leading one another
down the middle of the road — they look
like millions of armadillos or the stopped clocks
outside the mausoleum. I don't want to talk anymore,
I want to fuck and be fucked till I am
The Holiest Altar in America. Go!

Joel Lipman

. . .how many days have passed? Seven? Seven million?
Those oxen, rams, that olive oil, your long eyelashes,
kissing — I remember none of it.
You are here, I am not abandoned
in the middle of an hallucination.
My skin is still intact, I'm exhausted,
as if having slept weeks under the aquaduct.
I think we should get something to eat —
something other than burgers and pasta
and our own rarified bodies. Come, let's
steal a newspaper, spit in the gutter
and hide from the lousy soldiers.
Then we can duck into church and confess
or tie the knot and get married.

A Natural Death

Well, a poet
is a small boy and an old man,
the drunken diplomat of letters who works
for no-one and gives everything away.
The arabesque of neon is his red candle,
the laughter of that dying heart
his bare wood floor.
He dispenses everything.
Life is a quick song.
Look at them out there
touching the corpse while music
leaves those golden horns,

anything is possible—
the patio flares
are the flowers of ambulances,
and joy is the gasp of the crowd
when the ball clears the centerfield wall
in the last of the 12th.
A moment.
There is a bullfighter
dead in the sand
and an empty bed.
Everyone is walking away.

Contributors

CARRIE ALLEN was born in Chapel Hill, North Carolina and lives in Toledo's Old West End while pursuing graduate studies at the University of Toledo.

TOM BARDEN is a folklorist and Associate Professor of English at UT. His current book is *The Travels of Peter Woodhouse: Memoir of an American Pioneer* (Ocooch Mountain Press, 1981). A native Virginian, he lives with his wife and three sons in a house overlooking Swan Creek.

ALAN BASTING holds degrees from the University of Cincinnati, Colorado State University, and BGSU. A Rossford resident, he works as a technical writer for a Toledo corporation. A collection of poems, *What the Barns Breathe*, was published by Window Press in 1982.

MICHAEL BLAIR lives in the northwest Toledo neighborhood that was once the independent township of Trilby. Employed as a truck driver, he previously studied literature at the University of Toledo. He's recently been concentrating on prose.

WILLIAM BOTTORFF is Professor of English at the University of Toledo and a native of the city. His scholarly and creative publications include work in *Four Quarters*, *Cornfield Review*, and *Bitterroot*. He resides in Ottawa Hills.

STEVE CLARK is a Vietnam veteran and self-described "commercial criminal." He was an active member of the Toledo Poets Center's Inmate Arts Workshop in 1984.

PEGGIE CYPHER recently completed her first year of teaching at East Toledo Junior High School. An accomplished choreographer and dancer, she hails from the city's Point Place neighborhood, where a restaurant bears her family's name. This is her first published poem.

GEORGE deCHANT is a "firm believer that word processing is the wave of the future" and his self-produced, ephemeral publications reflect his interest in state-of-the-art technology. He studies theater at the University of Toledo.

LAWRENCE DESSNER is Professor of English at the University of Toledo, where his specialties include Victorian Literature and Creative Writing. His scholarship is published in the finest academic journals and his textbook, *How to Write a Poem* (NYU, 1979), has been acclaimed. Currently he is trying his hand at fiction.

A free-lance writer, SUE DWYER lives in Toledo. Her articles appear occasionally in *The Blade Magazine*.

MARIAN FISHER's poems will be published in 1985 by *The Mark*. She is a part-time instructor for UT's Department of English.

Since returning to the University of Toledo several years ago and earning her Master's in English, ZONA GALE has published a number of poems, been the dedicated editor of the *Mark*, written award-winning plays, two of which, "Walking" and "The Shower," were produced by the UT Department of Theater in 1985. Her editorship has made the *Mark* Toledo's leading literary periodical.

GUSTAVO (BUCHÉ) GARAY is a native Toledoan whose work has been published by *The Greenfield Review*. A prolific correspondent, Garay's mentor-in-absentia is Henry Miller.

E.R. GREGORY is Professor of English at the University of Toledo—among his specialties are Milton and detective fiction. Gregory's scholarship is published in a variety of academic journals and his latest book is *Milton and the Muses*. "I limit myself to writing light verse," is his comment upon his poetry.

ANNE PERRY GUIBERSON is a poet and painter. Co-founder of the Writers' Resource Center of Toledo, she's been a tireless promoter of the literary arts in the community.

ADAM HAMMER was an exuberant, handsome man who studied at BGSU and lived for a short while in Toledo. He died in 1984 following an automobile accident. His unusual, surrealistic poems were published by Lynx House Press in a book with the marvelous title *De'ja Everything*. *Glass Will* is dedicated to Hammer.

SIBYL JAMES lives in Washington and teaches English part-time at various Seattle-area colleges. A past member of the Seattle Arts Board, in 1985–86 she will teach English in Shanghai, China. James has performed her innovative translitics in Toledo. Her many publication credits include *Calyx, Michigan Quarterly Review, Ironwood* and *Tendril*.

JANE JOHANSON is a native of Scotland, Edinburgh University graduate, and Emerita Professor of Mathematics at the University of Toledo. Her two collections of poems are *Loving, Leaving & Living Again* and *Spirits and Seasons*.

BARBARA CLAIRE KASSELMANN works as a public relations and newsletter writer for a Toledo corporation. A graduate of Wright State University, she's a former Cincinnati resident. A number of her love poems were published in 1984 by the *Mark*.

ETHERIDGE KNIGHT is a distinguished poet who received a Guggenheim Fellowship in 1974. His published books include *Poems from Prison, Belly Song* and *Born of a Woman*. Born in Corinth, Mississippi in 1933, he lives in Philadelphia. His considerable influence upon Toledo poets results from many readings and residencies in the city. His papers are housed in the archives of the University of Toledo Canaday Center.

Raised in the northwest Ohio village of Berkey, ARNOLD KOESTER lives in Toledo's Old West End. "Just A Boy From Berkey" is his first published poem.

GAIL KONOP lives in New York City and teaches English at Park West High School in Manhattan. A Toledo native, she graduated with Honors from the University of Toledo and continued her studies at New York University.

JOEL LIPMAN edited *Glass Will*. From Wisconsin, he assumed a position on the University of Toledo faculty in 1975 and has lived here 10 years. Among his publications are two books of poems, *Mercury Vapor Lamp* and *Chicago You Got a Wide Stance*. Lipman is Director of the Toledo Poets Center.

DON McKIVETT studies theater at the University of Toledo. "The Garage-Father of Lambertville" is, as with many ballads, best sung.

PAUL MANY is Assistant Professor of Communication at the University of Toledo. His poems and short stories have been published in the little magazines *Uncle* and *Sequoya*. *Harbor of Sweet Losers* is his recently-completed first novel.

EUGENE MARINO formerly worked for *The Toledo Blade* and is currently a journalist in upstate New York.

HERBERT WOODWARD MARTIN is Professor of English at the University of Dayton. A Toledo native, he's published four volumes of poetry as well as critical work on Paul Laurence Dunbar. His papers are housed in the archives of the University of Toledo Canaday Center.

Retired and living in Holland, Ohio, RICHARD MORGEN-STERN is a member of the Dramatist's Guild and a free-lance writer.

Elm is NICK MUSKA's best-known book of poems. *Three Key West Sunsets* (Bloody Twin Press) is his most recently published work—it is an exquisite printing of three broadsides bound in handsome wrappers. A Loraine, Ohio, native, he studied at Antioch College, the University of California–Santa Barbara, and taught at Indiana's Wabash College. Married to a Toledoan, he's lived here since the early 1970s.

MARY ANN NAPOLEONE's avocation is poetry. A resident of suburban Toledo, she teaches part-time at UT and conducts poetry and prose workshops at the Writer's Resource Center of Toledo. A chapbook of her work was published in 1984 by the *Mark*.

JANE PIIRTO NAVARRE lives in New York City and is Principal of Hunter College Elementary School. A long-time Bowling Green resident, she holds a Ph.D. from BGSU. Her novel, *The Three-Week Trance Diet*, was published in 1986 by Carpenter Press. Navarre is currently Chairman of the Ohio Arts Council Literature Panel.

JEFF OLMA lives in Perrysburg and is a member of the Owens Technical College faculty. He holds an MFA from BGSU, has been a resident poet on the staff of the Ohio Arts Council Artist-in-the-Schools Program and has published poetry in distinguished literary periodicals. Portions of "The Wet Deck Poems" appeared earlier in *Salthouse*.

HOWARD T. PARKER is a voluminous writer of religious verse who starred in the Toledo House of Correction Writers' Workshop as an in-house poetry promoter.

RAY GENE PATRICK was born in Sciotoville, Ohio. A licensed hypnotherapist, he lives in Bradenton, Florida. For many years Patrick resided in Toledo.

JON PATTON is Director of Composition and Associate Professor of English at the University of Toledo. He is advisor for *Glass Review*, the University's literary magazine, and has had poems published in *Assembling* and *Akros*.

PAT PENCHEFF is a free-lance writer whose work, locally, has been published in *Toledo Alive* (now *Toledo* magazine). She studied literature at the University of Toledo and is a past winner of UT's student poetry competition.

BOB PHILLIPS composed his first poem when he was 12 and has been writing ever since. A lover of the solitude found on small lakes and ponds, he's an avid fisherman. A collection of his work, *I'm Not Your Sweet Babboo*, has been published in two editions by the Toledo Poets Center Press.

MARILYN LAYS PINHEIRO formerly taught at Medical College of Ohio. Handicapped for several years due to a spinal disease, she continues to write and has published a number of poems in *Spirits and Seasons*.

FRANK POLITE is from Youngstown, Ohio, lived for several years in the Toledo area, and currently teaches overseas for the University of Maryland—his work has taken him to Crete, Turkey, Germany and the Far East. *Letters of Transit* (City Miner) is his newest book. The Pangborn Press story remains to be told.

In 1965 DUDLEY RANDALL founded Broadside Press for the purpose of publishing work by young black poets. Since then, he's been central to the revival of Afro-American literature, winning numerous awards for his contributions as poet, editor, publisher and man of letters. Poet Laureate of Detroit, he resides in that city and has been an influential and generous supporter of Toledo poetry.

BRIAN RICHARDS grew up in Perrysburg and played basketball for PBHS. A BGSU graduate, for a number of years he's lived in the hill country along the Ohio River in Scioto County. His writing pops up in urbane, cosmopolitan literary journals and recent publications include work in *Exquisite Corpse* and *Rolling Stock*. Richards is the letterpress printer behind Bloody Twin Press.

JOHN GIBBS ROCKWOOD is a multi-talented artist. A bluesman, he's played harp with the finest musicians; his photographs of musicians are widely published; and if he can't sing, he sure can moan and wail. *Glass Will* is indebted to him for the original drawings used throughout the book. Another Toledo native.

DONNA ROWE participated in the Inmate Arts Program at the Lucas County Jail and the poem presented in this anthology is an outgrowth of those sessions. She was recently found guilty of murder by the State of South Carolina and sentenced to 150 to 300 years in prison.

HERB SCOTT has had an impact on Toledo poets because of his several readings and artist-in-the-schools residencies in the city. Among his books are *Dinosaurs*, *The Shoplifters Handbook*, and his latest, *Durations* (LSU Press, 1984).

A teacher and traveller in Asia, redoubtable conversationalist and memory-master, a man widely and curiously read, JOE SHEFFLER studied poetry at BGSU under Fred Eckman, holding degrees from that institution and the University of Massachusetts. *Manual For A 3-Day Mountain Walk* is printed here for the first time. Long a Wood County resident, Sheffler now lives in California.

SANDRA SMITH attends the University of Toledo and is completing work toward a Bachelor of Education degree in English. She lives in Toledo's Point Place neighborhood.

WINSTON SMITH, a retired Macomber High School teacher, lives in Lost Peninsula, Michigan. A veteran of World War II, he's been a flying instructor, aircraft mechanic, and president of the Toledo Poetry Society.

Poet and musician LAURIE SWYERS is employed by the Lucas County Children's Services Board. She lives west of Port Clinton, on the Lake Erie shore.

Now living in Cambridge, Massachusetts, and working at the poetry-famous Grollier's Bookstore, BOB TOMANSKI was a long-time Toledo kickabout, hospital worker and resident of the LaGrange neighborhood.

STEVE TOTH is a Toledo musician who has played drums for a number of area bands. Long employed by Doehler-Jarvis Corporation and active as a member of The Writers' Resource Center of Toledo, he has recently moved to Chicago.

PETER van SCHAICK lives in Toledo's Old West End. An art historian in academic background, his creative work includes arcane experimentation with rock sculpture, sound poetry and shamanism.

PAUL VARGO is an aspiring video artist who works with the Toledo Media Project. His work has been influenced by such intermedia pioneers as Tristan Tzara, Marcel DuChamp and Man Ray.

Born in Cuba and raised in Miami, MARISELLA VIEGA is a graduate of Macalester College and BGSU's MFA Program. Formerly a part-time instructor at the University of Toledo, she now lives in San Juan, Puerto Rico.

LYNNE WALKER has recently read her poems in Philadelphia and at the Maine Poetry Festival. Her innovative, bawdy, "Big Red" poems have been published in a variety of editions and periodicals. She's employed by the University of Toledo Department of Psychology.

MARGARET WEBER is an organist, pianist and composer, with degrees from the University of Michigan. She has taught at Mary Manse College and the University of Toledo. Accompanist for the Toledo Choral Society, her compositions have been performed by the Masterworks Chorale and the Toledo Orchestra Chorale.

Director of the Writer's Resource Center of Toledo, JOAN WERNERT, is at the center of Toledo's vital literary community. Formerly she operated the Colony Bookstore, the city's first shop specializing in independent and small press poetry publications. Her energy and generosity have turned an empty storefront into a prominent literary meetingplace. Wernert lives with her family in Ottawa Lake, Michigan.

MARTIN WILLITTS JR. is a Children's Librarian for the Toledo-Lucas County Public Library. He holds a Master's of Library Science from Syracuse University. Among his published works are 2 chapbooks, *The Circle is Never Broken* and *Exit Laughing*.

Recently married and moved to Amman, Jordan, WENDY WOOD is a native Toledoan and graduate of Vermont's Bennington College. Her poems are infrequently published, but an especially beautiful edition of "She-Leaves" was printed in 1980 as Tropos Press Broadside #3.